INGENIOUS MINDS: A TRIBUTE TO 100 GREAT SCIENTISTS AND INVENTORS

DR MONIM SHAH RAHMAN

Made with ♥ on the Notion Press Platform
www.notionpress.com

This book is dedicated to the brilliant minds whose curiosity, creativity and ingenuity have transformed our world. Their relentless pursuit of knowledge, groundbreaking discoveries and revolutionary inventions continue to inspire us all. May their remarkable achievements serve as a testament to the power of human intellect and the limitless possibilities of human endeavor.

Dr Monim Shah Rahman

Contents

Contents

Contents

Contents

Preface

In the annals of human history, there are those rare individuals who through their extraordinary insight, dedication and ingenuity have profoundly shaped the course of our civilization. From unraveling the mysteries of the Universe to revolutionizing the way we perceive the world around us, the contributions of these remarkable men and women have not only advanced our understanding of the universe but have also paved the way for the countless innovations that define the modern era. Ingenious Minds: A Tribute to 100 Great Scientists and Inventors is a celebration of the extraordinary achievements of some of history's most brilliant minds. In this volume, we pay homage to the visionary scientists and inventors whose groundbreaking discoveries and inventions have had a transformative impact on human welfare and progress.

From the revolutionary theories of Albert Einstein and the laws of motion formulated by Sir Isaac Newton to the heliocentric model of the universe proposed by Nicolaus Copernicus, these luminaries have reshaped our understanding of the natural world and expanded the boundaries of human knowledge.

Furthermore, we delve into the realm of biology, exploring the groundbreaking work of James Watson and Francis Crick whose discovery of the structure of DNA revolutionized the field of genetics and laid the foundation for modern biotechnology.

We also shine a light on the pioneering work of Max Planck, whose quantum theory transformed our understanding of the fundamental laws of physics and Nikola Tesla, whose innovative contributions to the field of electrical engineering continue to influence technology to this day.

Through their tireless pursuit of knowledge and unwavering commitment to discovery, these ingenious minds have left an indelible mark on the fabric of human history. It is our hope that this tribute serves as a testament to their enduring legacy and inspires future generations to continue pushing the boundaries of human knowledge.

Acknowledgements

This book, "Ingenious Minds: A Tribute to 100 Great Scientists and Inventors," would not have been possible without the unwavering support and inspiration of my beloved wife, Mrs Sabina Akter. Her brilliance in the field of Physics and Mathematics, and her relentless pursuit of knowledge have been a constant source of motivation for me.

Her insightful discussions, keen intellect and tireless encouragement have profoundly shaped this work. I would like to express my immense pleasure to acknowledge her patience and being my most dedicated critic. Her love and partnership have been my guiding force throughout this journey

With deepest gratitude and love.

Dr Monim Shah Rahman

Prologue

In the vast tapestry of human history, few threads have shaped our present and future as profoundly as the contributions of scientists and inventors. Their relentless curiosity, groundbreaking discoveries, and innovative creations have not only expanded the boundaries of our knowledge but have also transformed the way we live, think, and interact with the world. "Ingenious Minds: A Tribute to 100 Great Scientists and Inventors" is a celebration of these remarkable individuals who dared to dream beyond the ordinary and whose legacies continue to inspire generations.

Science and invention are the twin pillars of human progress. From the ancient sages who first mapped the stars to the modern-day pioneers pushing the frontiers of artificial intelligence, the quest for understanding and innovation has been a continuous and evolving journey. This book brings together the stories of 100 such visionaries, each of whom has left an indelible mark on our world. Their lives and works represent a diverse spectrum of disciplines, including physics, chemistry, biology, engineering, mathematics, and more. Among these luminaries, we encounter figures like Albert Einstein, whose theory of relativity revolutionized our understanding of space and time, and Marie Curie, whose pioneering research on radioactivity paved the way for significant advancements in medicine and atomic science. We delve into the minds of inventors like Nikola Tesla, whose innovations in electrical engineering have had a lasting impact on modern technology, and Ada Lovelace, whose visionary ideas laid the groundwork for computer programming.

Each chapter of this book is dedicated to a different scientist or inventor, offering a glimpse into their lives, their challenges, and their triumphs. We explore the context in which they worked, the obstacles they overcame, and the lasting implications of their contributions. Through their stories, we gain insight into the nature of scientific inquiry and the inventive process, marked by persistence, creativity, and a willingness to challenge the status quo.

It is essential to recognize that the journey of scientific discovery and invention is rarely a solitary endeavor. Collaboration, mentorship, and the exchange of ideas often play crucial roles in the breakthroughs that shape our world. This book also highlights the networks of influence and support that these great minds were part of, underscoring the interconnectedness of human achievement.

In celebrating these 100 great scientists and inventors, we also acknowledge the broader impact of their work on society. Scientific discoveries and technological innovations have the power to address some of the most pressing challenges of our time, from climate change and healthcare to communication and transportation. The stories in this book remind us of the potential for science and invention to drive progress and improve lives on a global scale. Moreover, "Ingenious Minds" seeks to inspire future generations to pursue their own paths of discovery and innovation. By learning about the experiences and contributions of these remarkable individuals, readers can find motivation and guidance in their own quests for knowledge and creativity. The legacy of these great minds serves as a testament to the profound difference that curiosity, determination, and ingenuity can make in the world.

In compiling this tribute, I have been deeply inspired by the brilliance and perseverance of these scientists and inventors. Their stories are a source of wonder and admiration, and I hope that this book will serve as a fitting homage to their extraordinary achievements. As we turn the pages and delve into the lives of these 100 ingenious minds, may we be reminded of the boundless possibilities that lie within the realm of human potential and the enduring power of scientific and inventive spirit.

Welcome to "Ingenious Minds: A Tribute to 100 Great Scientists and Inventors." Let us embark on this journey of exploration and celebration together.

CHAPTER ONE

SIR ISAAC NEWTON

Sir Isaac Newton was born on 4th January, 1643 in Woolsthorpe, England. He was a key persoality behind the 17th centuries scientific revolution and advancement.Through his significant ideas, he made foundation for contemporary Physics and Mathematics. The motion of things in the Universe was established by Newton in his great book "Philosophiae Naturalis Principia Mathematica" which was published in 1687 in which he was also introduced the law of universal gravitation. Newton's laws of motion define how forces interact with things in his fundamental principles of classical mechanics. His law of universal gravitation, a mathematical model for comprehending the motions of planets and other celestial bodies which describes how the masses attract one another in the universe.

In addition to physics, Newton made important contributions to astronomy, optics and mathematics. He established the foundation of calculus, the essential area of mathematics apart from Gottfried Wilhelm

Leibniz. Newton's discoveries and scientific achievements has altered our view of the natural world. His theories have an ever lasting impact on disciplines as diverse as physics, mathematics, astronomy and engineering which motivating many researchers and scientists to reach deeper into the hidden and unknown mysteries of the universe. The name of Isaac Newton is still associated with brilliance and intellectual curiosity.

CHARLES DARWIN

Charles Darwin was born on February 12, 1809 in Shrewsbury, England. He was a British naturalist and founder of the theory of evolution by natural selection, which transformed biology and our understanding of animals. The master piece "On the Origin of Species," which was written by Charles Darwin in 1859. The theory explains the chances of survival and reproduction increases for those most adapted species to their surroundings due to natural selection. Darwin's hypothesis, which contradicted conventional wisdom on the variety and origin of life was scientifically explained and the patterns seen in the fossil record and the global distribution of species. In the contemporary evolutionary biology, his theory received widespread support and served as the cornerstone. The theory initially generated a great deal of controversy and dispute.During his lifetime, Darwin carried out a great deal of study and observations which include the well known expedition he led on the HMS Beagle to the Galápagos Islands and gathered data in support theory of evolution.

The patterns seen in the fossil record and the global distribution of species were explained scientifically by Darwin's hypothesis, which contradicted conventional wisdom on the variety and origin of life. Over time, his theories received widespread support and served as the cornerstone of contemporary evolutionary biology, although they initially generated a great deal of controversy and dispute.

CHAPTER THREE

GALILEO GALILEI

Galileo Galilei was born on February 15, 1564 in Pisa, Italy. He was an physicist, astronomer and a mathematician. One of his significant contribution to science was the development of telescope and which made it possible for him to make revolutionary observations about astronomy. He discovered four moons of Jupiters in 1610 and today which were referred toas the Galilean moons.The heliocentric theory of the solar system explained by Copernicus' was supported by his findings. Apart from this, Galileo's discoveries challenged the existing Aristotelian cosmology and support the Copernican theory, which described that the Earth revolves around the Sun. As a result Conflict arose with the Catholic Church, condemning Galileo's heliocentric viewpoints. Galileo persisted in his scientific endeavors and make significant discoveries to the study of motion and development of the laws of inertia inspite of criticism.

The empirical method and mathematical analysis supported by Galileo transformed the scientific investigations and helped to open the door for the 17th-centuries scientific revolution. His contributions was significant for contemporary physics and astronomy which encouraged the new generations of researchers and scientists to challenge the conventional method and explore into the secrets of the galaxy. Galileo Galilei, renowned for his intellectual bravery and dedication to the search for truth, is still regarded as one of the key personality in the history of science.

CHAPTER FOUR

Nikola Tesla

Nikola Tesla was born on July 10, 1856, in Smiljan, Croatia, then was a part of the Austrian Empire. He was a physicist, an electrical engineer and a brilliant inventor. His discoveries had a significant impact on the advancement of contemporary technology. Tesla's groundbreaking research and the invention of alternating current (AC) electrical systems, wireless communication still influence the modern society. Tesla made significant advancement in the study of electricity and magnetism in the late 19th and early 20th century. His invention of the alternating current (AC) induction motor and the AC power transmission system make it possible for distribution and transfer of secure and efficient electrical energy across great distances. Additionally, Tesla make groundbreaking developments in wireless communication and radio technologies. His mission and vision of a society in such that information might be transferred wirelessly over long distances and which sparked the invention of technologies like radio transmission and remote control.

Tesla had many accomplishments over his scientific career but he was also faced financial and emotional difficulties. His fearless plans frequently went beyond the feasibility at that time, which leading him financial hardships and disagreements with investors.The name of Nikola Tesla is still associated with creativity, invention and the capacity for human imagination. His contributions to science, technology and society have left a everlasting impression on the contemporary world.

CHAPTER FIVE

LEONARDO DA VINCI

Leonardo da Vinci was born on April 15, 1452 in Vinci, Italy. He was a talented polymath and made contributions to art, engineering, science and anatomy. He represents the idea of the Renaissance and is considered to be one of the greatest geniuses of all time. da Vinci's masterworks, such as "Mona Lisa," and "The Last Supper" are praised for his inventive methods, emotional depth, and technical skill. As a consequence of his rigorous research of human anatomy and keen observation of nature, he created remarkably expressive and lifelike depictions of the human form and the natural environment. Apart from a brilliant artist, Da Vinci was also a brilliant inventor and an engineer. He showed an unmatched understanding of inventive thinking and mechanical principles by designing armored vehicles, flying aircraft, and hydraulic systems in advance form of his time.

Leonardo da Vinci experimented with a variety of subjects, including astronomy, mathematics, geology and botany because of his boundless curiosity and vast imagination. His note books are still an inspiration of today's artists, scientists and thinkers because they are crammed with sketches, diagrams and observations that give us a glimpse into his amazing intellect. The Renaissance genius Leonardo da Vinci is regarded as living legend of multidisciplinary thinking, imagination in the search for knowledge and curiosity.

CHAPTER SIX

ARISTOTLE

Aristotle was born around 384 BC in Stagira, Greece. He was one of the most notable philosopher and scientist in history. while he was a student, he was one of the most well-known pupils of Plato. Aristotle made extensive contributions to a variety of fields, including biology, physics, logic, politics, ethics, and philosophy. Aristotle wrote on almost every topic under the sun in philosophy. He created the extensive reasoning system known as Aristotelian logic, which had a long-lasting impact. In terms of politics, he examined several systems of governance and argued for a hybrid constitution that would strike a balance between democracy and oligarchy.

Aristotle also conducted extensive scientific research. His discoveries and classifications in biology provided the groundwork in the fields of botany and zoology. His theory of motion and his conception of potentiality and actuality are only two of the many important contributions he made to physics. The writings of Aristotle, such as "Metaphysics," "Physics," "Politics," and "Nicomachean Ethics," among others, have had a significant and enduring influence on Western philosophy. His focus on methodical investigation, logical reasoning, and empirical observation set the foundation for the scientific method and influenced the course of Western philosophy and science for centuries to come. Aristotle is regarded as one of the most influential thinkers in intellectual history because of his lasting effect on a variety of disciplines, including politics, biology, ethics, and metaphysics.

CHAPTER SEVEN

Max Planck

Max Planck was born on April 23, 1858 in Kiel, Germany. He was a great physicist whose work transformed our understanding of the fundamental rules of nature. His contribution to the development of quantum theory which served as the basis for contemporary physics made him most famous. Planck proposed the idea of quantization in 1900 and arguing that energy is not continually released or absorbed but rather occurs in discrete packets known as "quanta." This ground-breaking theory provided an explanation for the black-body radiation spectrum that was seen and addressed the long-standing ultraviolet catastrophe issue in classical physics. Planck's discovery of quantum theory changed the course of physics and opened the door for more advancement in the field of quantum mechanics. His contributions had a broad impact on a variety of disciplines including solid-state physics, particle physics, atomic and nuclear physics.

Planck made important contributions to theoretical physics and thermodynamics in addition to his revolutionary investigations. For his contributions to the quantum theory, he received the Nobel Prize in Physics in 1918. Our view of the the universe is still shaped by Max Planck, the visionary scientist and pioneer. The spirit of inquiry and discovery that propels scientific advancement is embodied in his willingness to challenge received information and venture into unexplored scientific territory. Planck is expected to have an influence on physics for many years to come as his discoveries are still essential to our current understanding of the universe.

CHAPTER EIGHT

Marshall Warren Nirenberg

Marshall Warren Nirenberg was born on April 10, 1927, in New York City. He was an American biochemist who was awarded the Nobel Prize in Physiology or Medicine in 1968. Nirenberg's groundbreaking research laid the foundation for our understanding of how the genetic code controls the synthesis of proteins within cells. Nirenberg's most famous achievement came in 1961 when, along with his colleague Heinrich Matthaei, he conducted an experiment that deciphered the first codon of the genetic code. By synthesizing RNA molecules made up of a single type of nucleotide, they were able to determine that the genetic code is composed of three nucleotide sequences called codons, each of which specifies a particular amino acid.

This discovery opened the door to further research into the genetic code, paving the way for advances in molecular biology and biotechnology. In 1968, Nirenberg was awarded the Nobel Prize in Physiology or Medicine for his contributions to this field. Throughout his career, Nirenberg made numerous other important contributions to molecular biology including research on the regulation of gene expression and the role of RNA in protein synthesis. He continued to conduct research until his death on January 15, 2010, leaving behind a legacy of groundbreaking discoveries that have had a profound impact on our understanding of genetics and molecular biology.

CHAPTER NINE

GEORGE STEPHENSON

George Stephenson, often hailed as the "Father of Railways," was a pioneering figure whose innovations revolutionized transportation during the Industrial Revolution. Born on June 9, 1781, in Wylam, Northumberland, England. Stephenson's childhood was marked by poverty, and he received little formal education. At the age of eight, he began working at a local coal mine where he learned about steam engines. Despite his lack of formal education, Stephenson's innate curiosity and keen interest in mechanics led him to become an expert in steam powered machinery. In 1814, Stephenson built his first locomotive, the Blücher for the Killingworth Colliery railway. This locomotive was a significant improvement over existing models with its innovative design allowing it to haul heavy loads more efficiently. Stephenson's success caught the attention of the colliery's owner Lord Ravensworth, who provided him with the resources to further develop his ideas. In 1825, Stephenson built the world's first successful steam powered railway locomotive, the "Locomotion No. 1." This locomotive was designed for the Stockton and Darlington Railway, which was the first public railway to use steam locomotives.

Stephenson's "Locomotion No. 1" was a significant leap forward in railway technology. It was faster, more reliable, and more efficient than previous models and it quickly proved its worth by hauling coal and passengers along the Stockton and Darlington Railway. In 1829, Stephenson achieved his greatest success with the invention of the "Rocket." The "Rocket" was built for the Rainhill Trials, a competition to find the best locomotive for the Liverpool and Manchester Railway. The "Rocket" was a marvel of engineering with its innovative design incorporating a number of important features, including a multi tubular boiler, a blast pipe and a separate firebox.

CHAPTER TEN

Daniel Bernoulli

Daniel Bernoulli was born on February 8, 1700, in Groningen, Netherlands. He was a distinguished Swiss mathematician and physicist renowned for his contributions to fluid dynamics and the kinetic theory of gases. He hailed from the illustrious Bernoulli family, which produced several prominent mathematicians. Bernoulli is most celebrated for formulating Bernoulli's principle, a fundamental theorem in fluid mechanics. Bernoulli's principle introduced in his 1738 work "Hydrodynamica," states that an increase in the speed of a fluid results in a decrease in its pressure or potential energy. This principle is crucial for understanding various phenomena including the lift on airplane wings, the behavior of natural waterways and the function of pumps and turbines.

Beyond fluid dynamics, Bernoulli made significant strides in probability and statistics, exploring concepts of risk and utility that laid the groundwork for expected utility theory. His interdisciplinary approach extended to medicine, where he applied mathematical analysis to physiological processes such as blood flow and cardiac function. Bernoulli's work exemplified the integration of mathematical principles with practical applications, influencing numerous scientific fields. He died on March 17, 1782, in Basel, Switzerland. His legacy endures through the many scientific principles bearing his name, underscoring his lasting impact on mathematics, physics and engineering.

CHAPTER ELEVEN

RICHARD FEYNMAN

Richard Feynman was born on May 11, 1918 in Queens, New York. He was a great theoretical physicist. He is well-known for his outstanding contributions to particle physics, quantum mechanics, and quantum electrodynamics (QED). Feynman is known as one of the most influential physicists of the 20th century due to his novel approach to physics, which was marked by his humorous curiosity and intuitive insights. Together with Julian Schwinger and Sin-Itiro Tomonaga, Feynman received the Nobel Prize in Physics in 1965 for his outstanding contributions to the development of quantum electrodynamics. His representations of particle interactions or Feynman diagrams revolutionized the science and provided a potent tool for computing complex quantum processes.

Feynman was not just a brilliant theoretical physicist but also a superb teacher and communicator. Generations of scientists and students have been inspired by his lectures, which are well recognized for their humor, intelligence, and clarity. These lectures include the well-known "Feynman

Lectures on Physics." Beyond physics, Feynman's boundless curiosity and innovative approach to problem-solving were noteworthy. In addition, he was a skilled artist, safecracker, and bongo musician. He was well-liked in the scientific community and beyond because of his vibrant personality and boundless energy. The lasting impact of physicist, educator, and visionary thinker Richard Feynman is still inspiring and influencing scientists and educators around the world.

CHAPTER TWELVE

JAMES CLERK MAXWELL

James Clerk Maxwell was born on June 13, 1831 in Edinburgh, Scotland. He was a pioneering physicist whose work established the groundwork for contemporary electromagnetic and theoretical physics. By combining electricity, magnetism, and light into a unified theoretical framework Maxwell's revolutionary equations—also referred to as Maxwell's equations—radically altered our understanding of these three phenomena. Maxwell's most important contribution was the creation of the theory of electromagnetism. He published a series of equations describing the interaction and propagation of electriomagnetic waves in space in the 1860s. The theory behind the creation of technologies like radio, television, and radar was based on these equations, which proved that light is an electromagnetic wave.

Apart from his contributions to electromagnetism, Maxwell also made significant advancement in thermodynamics and the kinetic theory of gases. He established the Maxwell distribution concept, which determines the distribution of particle velocities in a gas, and he mathematically explained the principles of thermodynamics. Maxwell's fundamental discoveries on the nature of light, eletricity and magnetism established the foundation for modern physics. As one of the greatest physicists of all time, he left behind equations that are still among the most sophisticated and significant in scientific history and his contributions to science continue to inspire and guide scientific inquiry and advancement.

CHAPTER THIRTEEN

JOHANNES KEPLER

Johannes Kepler was born on December 27, 1571, in Weil der Stadt, Holy Roman Empire (now Germany). He was a pioneering mathematician and astronomer whose work revolutionized our knowledge of the universe. Our understanding of the solar system was completely changed by Kepler's equations of planetary motion, which also served as the cornerstone for modern astronomy. Kepler's first law, the law of elliptical orbits, stated that the planets move around the Sun in elliptical paths rather than perfect circles. This departure from the prevailing belief in circular orbits was a monumental breakthrough in celestial mechanics.

His second law, the law of equal areas, demonstrated that planets sweep out equal areas in equal time by describing the speed at which they move in their orbits. Important insights into the mechanics of planetary motion were given by this law. According to Kepler's third law, the law of harmonies, the orbital periods and separations of planets from the Sun are precisely correlated mathematically. Isaac Newton's law of universal gravity was made possible by this law, which also enabled astronomers to determine the relative diameters of planetary orbits. Kepler made important contributions to astronomy as well as mathematics and optics. His work served as a link between the scientific traditions of the medieval and modern periods and his detailed observations and mathematical analysis prepared the way for the 17th-century scientific revolution. The pioneering work of Johannes Kepler, as a mathematician and astronomer continues to motivate researchers and scientists to discover the mysteries of the universe.

CHAPTER FOURTEEN

DMITRI MENDELEEV

Famous chemist Dmitri Mendeleev was born on February 8, 1834 in Tobolsk, Siberia, Russian Empire (now Russia). He is best known for developing the periodic table of elements. His ground-breaking work revolutionized chemistry and offered a methodical framework for understanding the characteristics of the elements. Mendeleev's periodic chart exhibited remarkable patterns and linkages by grouping the known elements according to their atomic mass and chemical characteristics into rows and columns. Using the patterns seen in elements that had already been identified, he predicted the properties of the elements that were yet to be discovered and left spaces in his table for them. This foresight led to the discovery of several new elements, validating the predictive power of his periodic table.

Mendeleev made important contributions to the study of gases, solutions and the theory of chemical equilibrium in addition to his work on the periodic table. He proposed the concept of the periodic law which states that the properties of the elements vary periodically with their atomic number. Mendeleev's contributions to chemistry and education are still honored today. His periodic table which offers a framework for arranging and analyzing the characteristics of the elements is still regarded as one of the most significant tools in chemistry. Chemistry and science as a whole have been profoundly impacted by Mendeleev's methodology for research, theoretical reasoning and dedication to practical observation.

CHAPTER FIFTEEN

WERNER HEISENBERG

Werner Heisenberg was born on December 5, 1901, in Würzburg, Germany. He was a pioneering physicist who made profound contributions to quantum mechanics and theoretical physics. His most famous contribution to science was the establishment of the uncertainty principle, which completely altered our understanding of how subatomic particles behave. The exact position and momentum of a particle cannot be known with absolute confidence at the same time according to Heisenberg's uncertainty principle, which was established in 1927. This principle introduced a fundamental limit to the precision with which certain pairs of physical properties can be measured leading to a radical shift in the conceptual framework of quantum mechanics.

Apart from his work on the uncertainty principle, Heisenberg made significant contributions to the development of matrix mechanics, a mathematical model that provided a powerful tool for describing the behavior of quantum systems. In addition, he was actively engaged in the advancement of particle physics and quantum field theory. Numerous further developments in theoretical physics, such as the development of quantum electrodynamics and the standard model of particle physics were made possible by Heisenberg's work. He was awarded the Nobel Prize in Physics in 1932 for his contributions to the development of quantum mechanics.

CHAPTER SIXTEEN

LOUIS PASTEUR

Louis Pasteur was born on December 27, 1822, in Dole, France. He was a pioneering chemist and microbiologist whose discoveries revolutionized medicine and biology. His contributions to the fields of pasteurization and vaccination as well as his work in inventing the germ theory of illness have earned him the most recognition. Pasteur's research challenged the widely held notion that spontaneous creation occurs spontaneously by showing that microbes are the root cause of many ailments. His work served as a precursor to the germ theory of disease which revolutionized our knowledge of the origins of infectious illnesses and sparked the development of vaccines and antibiotics. In addition, Pasteur is recognized for having created vaccinations against a number of fatal illnesses such as anthrax and rabies. His vaccine research established the fundamentals of immunology and saved many lives. Apart from his discovery in vaccines and immunology, Pasteur achieved significant improvements to the discipline of chemistry. He made the fundamental discoveries of chirality and molecular asymmetry which established the foundation for stereochemistry.

Today, Pasteur's contributions to science and innovation are still honored. His findings have had a significant influence on industry, agriculture and public health. His approaches to scientific investigation and testing are still fundamental to the conduct of contemporary research. The life and work of Louis Pasteur serve as an excellent example of the value of thorough investigation and the strength of scientific inquiry in expanding our knowledge of the natural world.

CHAPTER SEVENTEEN

LINUS PAULING

Linus Pauling was born on February 28, 1901, in Portland, Oregon. He was a towering figure in 20th-century science, renowned for his groundbreaking contributions to chemistry, molecular biology and peace activism. He remains the only individual to have been awarded two unshared Nobel Prizes, one in Chemistry in 1954 and another for Peace in 1962. Pauling's discoveries on the nature of chemical bonds transformed our knowledge of molecular structure and served as a precursor to contemporary quantum chemistry. One of the most important scientific publications of the 20th century is said to be his book "The Nature of the Chemical Bond". Pauling made important contributions to molecular biology and medicine as a result of his interest in biology.

In addition to his scientific achievements, Pauling was a passionate advocate for peace and nuclear disarmament. He co-founded the International League of Humanists and the Nobel Peace Prize-winning organization, the Pugwash Conferences on Science and World Affairs which aimed to reduce the threat of nuclear war through dialogue and diplomacy. Generations of scientists and activists are still motivated to utilize their expertise and influence for the benefit of mankind and the wider world by Linus Pauling's legacy as a scientist, humanitarian and peace campaigner.

CHAPTER EIGHTEEN

ERWIN SCHRODINGER

Erwin Schrodinger was born on August 12, 1887, in Vienna, Austria-Hungary (now Austria). He was a pioneering physicist who made significant contributions to the development of quantum mechanics. The development of the Schrodinger equation which explains how a physical system's quantum state varies over time and which made him most famous. The behavior of atoms and subatomic particles may be predicted using Schrodinger's equation which is essential to quantum mechanics. It is a representation of a wave equation that explains a particle's wave function and presents a theoretical foundation for interpreting concepts, like quantum superposition and wave-particle duality.

Apart from his contributions to the Schrodinger equation, Schrodinger had a significant role in the understanding of quantum mechanics. He is credited for proposing the thought experiment known as "Schrodinger's cat," which exemplifies the purpose of observation in quantum measurement and the idea of quantum superposition. Schrodinger and Paul Dirac shared the 1933 Nobel Prize in Physics for the development of the

Schrodinger equation, which pioneering research served as the basis for several other advancements in quantum physics. His name is closely associated with the foundational ideas of quantum mechanics and his contributions to the discipline are still honored today.

CHAPTER NINETEEN

ALBERT EINSTEIN

Albert Einstein was born on March 14, 1879, in Ulm, Germany. He was a theoretical physicist. He had a profound impact on our knowledge of the univers. Following his schooling in Switzerland, Einstein began his career as a patent examiner in Bern, where he worked on the ideas that would later become known as relativity and the equivalency of mass and energy. Known as his "annus mirabilis" or "miracle year," 1905 saw the publication of four ground-breaking works by him, among them his theory of special relativity, which gave rise to the well-known equation $E=mc2$, which illustrates the link between mass and energy. Modern cosmology and astrophysics have been greatly impacted by Einstein's theory of general relativity which was published in 1915 and offered a novel interpretation of gravity as the curvature of spacetime. He received the Nobel Prize in Physics in 1921 for his description of the photoelectric effect.

Einstein arrived in the United States as a refugee from Nazi persecution, where he was employed as a professor at Princeton, New Jersey's Institute for Advanced Study. He stayed an influential scientist and a supporter of social justice and peace for the duration of his life. Future generations of physicists and intellectuals throughout the world are continually motivated by Einstein's legacy as one of the world's greatest scientists.

CHAPTER TWENTY

MARIE CURIE

Marie Curie was born on November 7, 1867, as Maria Skłodowska in Warsaw, Poland. She was a pioneering chemist and physicist who made significant advancements in the study of radioactivity. As a woman in science at that time, Curie faced many obstacles, yet her intelligence and willpower propelled her to remarkable success. Curie went to Paris in 1891 to pursue her education at the Sorbonne, where she eventually married fellow scientist Pierre Curie in 1895. They collaborated to carry out groundbreaking research on radioactivity, a word they used to characterize the radiation that some materials spontaneously emit.

Together with Pierre and Henri Becquerel, Marie Curie was the first woman to receive the Nobel Prize in Chemistry in 1903 for their research on radioactivity. In 1911, she achieved another piece of history when she was awarded the first-ever double Nobel Prize in Chemistry for discovering the elements radium and polonium. Because of her gender, Curie encountered discrimination and distrust from certain members of the scientific community despite her ground-breaking findings. Nevertheless, she made indisputable contributions to science and her legacy as a legendary figure in physics and chemistry lives on. Around the world, women in STEM areas are still motivated by Marie Curie's legacy which highlights the value of tenacity, intelligence and devotion to scientific research.

CHAPTER TWENTY-ONE

PAUL DIRAC

Paul Dirac was born on August 8, 1902, in Bristol, England, was a pioneering figure in theoretical physics, whose ground breaking work laid the foundation for much of modern quantum mechanics and quantum electrodynamics. His father, Charles Dirac, a Swiss-born French teacher, and his mother, Florence Holten, fostered a strict and disciplined environment that significantly influenced Dirac's personality and work ethic. Dirac's most celebrated contribution is the Dirac equation, formulated in 1928. This relativistic wave equation describes the behavior of fermions, such as electrons, and successfully merges quantum mechanics with special relativity. The Dirac equation predicted the existence of antimatter, specifically the positron, which was experimentally confirmed by Carl Anderson in 1932. This discovery was pivotal, as it expanded the understanding of particle physics and led to significant advancements in the field.. He introduced the braket notation, which became a fundamental tool in quantum mechanics, simplifying complex equations and making the abstract concepts more accessible.

In 1933, Dirac was awarded the Nobel Prize in Physics, which he shared with Erwin Schrödinger, for the discovery of new productive forms of atomic theory. Despite his monumental achievements, Dirac was known for his terse and precise communication style, both in speech and writing. His reticence and unconventional personality earned him the nickname "the strangest man" in physics, a term popularized by biographer Graham Farmelo. Dirac held the prestigious Lucasian Chair of Mathematics at the University of Cambridge from 1932 until his retirement in 1969, a position once held by Sir Isaac Newton.

CHAPTER TWENTY-TWO

ROBERT HOOKE

Robert Hooke was born on July 18, 1635, in Freshwater, Isle of Wight. He was a brilliant scientist and polymath known for his contributions to a wide range of fields, including physics, astronomy, biology and architecture. Hooke's keen observational skills, innovative experiments and inventive mind made him one of the most influential figures of the scientific revolution. Hooke is perhaps best known for his work in microscopy and his discovery of the cellular structure of living organisms. In his seminal work "Micrographia," published in 1665, Hooke described and illustrated his observations of various natural phenomena under the microscope including the intricate structure of cork cells which he likened to the small rooms or "cells" in a monastery.

In addition to his work in microscopy, Hooke made significant contributions to the fields of physics and astronomy. He formulated Hooke's law which describes the relationship between the force exerted on a spring and the displacement of the spring and he made important discoveries in optics, gravitation and planetary motion. Hooke's impact on the scientific community extended beyond his own research. He was a founding member and curator of the Royal Society of London where he played a key role in promoting scientific inquiry and collaboration. His legacy as a pioneering scientist and thinker continues to be celebrated today and his contributions to the advancement of knowledge.

CHAPTER TWENTY-THREE

ANTONIE VAN LEEUWENHOEK

Antonie van Leeuwenhoek was born on October 24, 1632, in Delft, Netherlands. He was a Dutch scientist and tradesman who is often referred to as the "Father of Microbiology." Despite having no formal scientific education, Leeuwenhoek made groundbreaking discoveries in the field of microscopy and laid the foundation for the study of microbiology. Leeuwenhoek's interest in microscopy was sparked by his work as a draper where he used magnifying lenses to examine the quality of cloth fibers. Using handcrafted microscopes of his own design. Leeuwenhoek made detailed observations of a wide range of microscopic organisms including bacteria, protozoa and sperm cells.

In 1676, Leeuwenhoek reported his discovery of "animalcules" in samples of water from various sources which he observed to be teeming with tiny living creatures. His meticulous observations and accurate drawings of these microorganisms provided crucial evidence for the existence of microscopic life and helped to overturn the prevailing belief in spontaneous generation. Leeuwenhoek's discoveries revolutionized our understanding of the natural world and paved the way for the field of microbiology. His innovative use of microscopy and his rigorous approach to scientific inquiry continue to inspire researchers and scientists to this day. Antonie van Leeuwenhoek's contributions to the advancement of science and medicine have earned him a lasting place in the annals of scientific history.

CHAPTER TWENTY-FOUR

MICHAEL FARADAY

Michael Faraday was born on September 22, 1791, in Newington Butts, Surrey, England. He was one of the most influential scientists of the 19th century known for his pioneering work in the fields of electromagnetism and electrochemistry. Despite humble beginnings Faraday's insatiable curiosity and innate talent for experimental science propelled him to become one of the greatest experimental physicists of his time. Faraday's most significant contributions came in the field of electromagnetism. In 1831, he discovered electromagnetic induction demonstrating that a changing magnetic field can induce an electric current in a nearby conductor. This discovery laid the foundation for the modern electric generator and transformer which revolutionizing the field of electrical engineering and powering the Industrial Revolution.

In addition to his work on electromagnetism, Faraday made important contributions to the understanding of electrolysis and the nature of electricity and magnetism. His experiments with electrolysis led to the development of Faraday's laws of electrolysis, which describe the quantitative relationship between the amount of substance deposited during electrolysis and the electric current passed through the electrolyte. Faraday's legacy as a scientist, inventor and educator is immense. His discoveries and insights have had a profound impact on the development of modern technology and science and his innovative approach to experimental science continues to inspire generations of scientists and engineers. Michael Faraday's pioneering work laid the groundwork for much of our modern understanding of electromagnetism and continues to shape the world we live in

CHAPTER TWENTY-FIVE

STEPHEN HAWKING

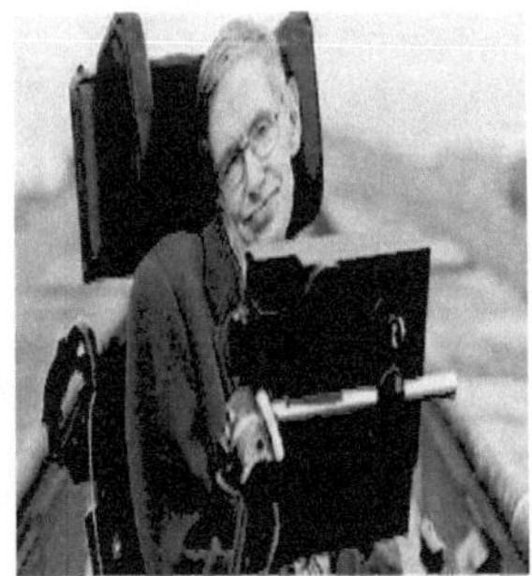

Stephen Hawking was born on January 8, 1942, in Oxford, England. He was a theoretical physicist. His research on black holes, cosmology and the nature of the universe gained the attention of people all around the world. Even after receiving an ALS diagnosis at age 21, Hawking exceeded expectations by carrying out ground-breaking research and rising to prominence among scientists of his period. The hypothesis of Hawking radiation, which postulates that black holes may emit radiation and progressively lose mass over time is Hawking's most well-known contribution. This idea has significant implications for our understanding of the universe and contradicted traditional views on black holes.

Along with his scientific achievements, Hawking was a prolific writer and science communicator who helped laypeople to understand difficult subjects. The worldwide success of his book "A Brief History of Time" established his reputation as a cultural icon. Millions of people worldwide were inspired by Hawking's intelligence, humor and determination despite his physical limitations. Throughout his life, he was honored with a great deal of recognition, such as the Presidential Medal of Freedom and at the age of thirty-two, he was made a Fellow of the Royal Society. As a gifted scientist, orator and representation of human tenacity, Stephen Hawking's contribution will motivate next generations to investigate deeper into the secrets of the universe and expand the frontiers of human understanding.

CHAPTER TWENTY-SIX

NIELS BOHR

Niels Bohr was born on October 7, 1885 in Copenhagen, Denmark. He was a Danish physicist who made significant contributions to our knowledge of atomic structure and quantum theory. He is most known for creating the Bohr model of the atom which revolutionised physics in the early twentieth century. Bohr introduced his concept in 1913 combining classical mechanics with the new subject of quantum mechanics. He proposed that electrons move around the nucleus of an atom in discrete, defined energy levels rather than in continuous orbits as previously understood. This model accurately described hydrogen's spectral lines and gave a foundation for understanding atom. Bohr's work set the groundwork for present knowledge of atomic and subatomic structures and he was a key figure in the development of quantum theory. He was awarded the Nobel Prize in Physics in 1922 for his contributions to the study of atomic structure and quantum mechanics.

Throughout his life, Bohr was a prominent figure in the scientific community pushing for international collaboration and the peaceful use of nuclear energy. His impact continues to shape physics and motivate scientists to uncover the secrets of the quantum world.

52

CHAPTER TWENTY-SEVEN

AHMED ZEWAIL

Ahmed Zewail was born on February 26, 1946, in Damanhur, Egypt. He was an Egyptian American scientist who won the Nobel Prize in Chemistry in 1999 for his pioneering work on femtochemistry, the study of chemical reactions on extremely short timescales. Zewail's interest in science was evident from an early age. He earned his bachelor's and master's degrees from Alexandria University before pursuing his Ph.D at the University of Pennsylvania. Zewail's groundbreaking work revolutionized the field of chemistry by allowing scientists to observe the behavior of molecules in real-time on timescales of femtoseconds (one millionth of one billionth of a second). Using a technique called ultrafast laser spectroscopy and Zewail was able to capture images of molecules as they underwent chemical reactions providing unprecedented insights into the fundamental processes that govern chemistry.

In addition to his Nobel Prize, Zewail received numerous awards and honors throughout his career including the Albert Einstein World Award of Science and the Priestley Medal, the highest honor awarded by the American Chemical Society. He was also appointed to numerous scientific advisory boards and served as a science envoy for President Barack Obama. Zewail's work has had a profound impact on our understanding of chemistry and has opened up new possibilities for the design of novel materials and drugs. He passed away on 2nd August, 2016, leaving behind a legacy of scientific achievement and innovation.

CHAPTER TWENTY-EIGHT

ALAN TURING

Alan Turing was born on June 23, 1912, in London, England. He was a mathematician, logician, and pioneering computer scientist. He is recognized by many as the founder of artificial intelligence and theoretical computer science. Turing's innovative work changed the direction of World War II and established a foundation for contemporary computers. Turing was instrumental in the war effort helping to reduce the duration and save many lives by cracking the German Enigma code. His leadership of a group of codebreakers at Bletchley Park helped decode intercepted German transmissions and gave the Allies vital intelligence.

Turing continued to making important contributions to computer science after the war. He created the theoretical Turing machine idea which served as the foundation for the development of the contemporary digital computer. In addition, Turing developed the Turing test, a procedure for judging if a machine is intelligent enough to be considered human. Turing has been honored posthumously in recent years for his services to science and society. Queen Elizabeth II pardoned him majestically in 2013 and the new £50 note in the UK honors him. The work of Alan Turing the brilliant mathematician, codebreaker and pioneer of computers is still an inspiration to future generations of engineers and scientists.

CHAPTER TWENTY-NINE

ROSALIND FRANKLIN

Rosalind Franklin was born on July 25, 1920, in London, England. She was an innovative chemist and X-ray crystallographer. Her work was essential in determining the structure of DNA. Franklin's pioneering study lay the foundation for one of the greatest discoveries in biology, while enduring prejudice based on gender in the male-dominated scientific world of the mid-20th century. Franklin joined the team at King's College London in 1951 and studied the structure of DNA fibers using X-ray diffraction methods. Her careful research resulted in excellent X-ray pictures, such as Photograph 51, which gave significant fresh data on the helical structure of DNA. Unknown to Franklin, James Watson and Francis Crick shared Photograph 51 at the Cavendish Laboratory in Cambridge with her colleague Maurice Wilkins. Franklin's results helped Watson and Crick to develop their well-known double helix model of DNA, which they published in 1953. They also used other experimental evidence.

Franklin had a crucial part in the discovery of the DNA structure, although her efforts were not entirely acknowledged at the time of her death. Sadly, she died in 1958 at the age of 37 from ovarian cancer, before the importance of her work was generally recognized. Franklin's contributions to science have gained more attention in the decades after her passing and she is now honored as an inspiration for women in STEM disciplines. Her work serves as a constant reminder of the value of determination, morality and superior scientific achievement in the search for knowledge.

CHAPTER THIRTY

CARL SAGAN

Carl Sagan was born on November 9, 1934, in Brooklyn, New York. He was an American astronomer, cosmologist, author and scientific communicator who. He has a significant personality in bringing science to the general public and in making difficult scientific ideas understandable. Sagan captivated the attention of millions of people worldwide with his enthusiasm for astronomy and his ability to explain the wonders of the the universe. Sagan made important advances in the fields of astrobiology and planetary science. He was involved in the design and implementation of the Golden Record inside the Voyager spacecraft, which contains sounds and pictures depicting Earth's biodiversity and culture as well as the Mariner, Viking, Voyager and Galileo space missions.

Sagan was a prolific writer who produced a number of best-selling books, such as "Cosmos," which went along with his innovative "Cosmos" television series. The capacity of "Cosmos" to successfully combine science, philosophy, history and art led to it being one of the most viewed shows in the history of public television. A long-lasting legacy was left by Sagan's support of critical thinking, scientific skepticism and the hunt for alien intelligence. He served as an inspiration to countless numbers of scientists, educators and scientific enthusiasts to investigate the mysteries of the universe and to approach the problems that face mankind with reason, compassion and curiosity. People all throughout the world are still motivated and educated by Carl Sagan's ongoing influence, which serves as a constant reminder of the value of scientific research and the infinite possibilities of the universe.

CHAPTER THIRTY-ONE

EDWIN HUBBLE

American astronomer Edwin Hubble was born on November 20, 1889, in Marshfield, Missouri. His contributions greatly expanded our knowledge of the universe and our role within it. Finding evidence of the universe's expansion was Hubble's most important contribution. Hubble began observing galaxies far away in the 1920s and discovered that they were migrating away from Earth with the newly constructed 100-inch Hooker Telescope at Mount Wilson Observatory in California. This discovery led to the formulation of Hubble's Law, which states that the farther away a galaxy is from us, the faster it is moving away. The Big Bang hypothesis, which postulates that the universe started as a hot, dense singularity and has been expanding ever since, was supported by strong evidence from Hubble's observations. His contributions significantly altered our comprehension of cosmology and established the foundation for contemporary cosmological ideas. Apart from his innovative studies, Hubble was instrumental in the advancement of extragalactic astronomy and the categorization of galaxies. In his honor, the Hubble Space Telescope was put into orbit in 1990 and has since contributed significantly to our understanding of the universe.

Scientists and enthusiasts people are still motivated by Edwin Hubble's legacy as a visionary astronomer and cosmologist, which serves as a constant reminder of the universe's vastness, complexity and our never-ending search to solve its secrets.

CHAPTER THIRTY-TWO

AZIZ SANCAR

Aziz Sancar was Born on September 8, 1946, in Savur, Turkey, is a Turkish-American biochemist who was awarded the Nobel Prize in Chemistry in 2015 for his mechanistic studies of DNA repair. Sancar's interest in science was nurtured from a young age. He earned his medical degree from Istanbul University in 1969 before pursuing a Ph.D in molecular biology at the University of Texas at Dallas. Sancar's research has focused primarily on understanding the mechanisms by which cells repair DNA damage caused by exposure to ultraviolet (UV) light and other environmental factors. His work has led to significant advancements in our understanding of DNA repair processes and their implications for health and disease. One of Sancar's most significant contributions to science was his discovery of the mechanisms behind nucleotide excision repair (NER), a fundamental process that cells use to repair DNA damage caused by UV radiation. By identifying the proteins involved in NER and elucidating the biochemical steps of the repair process, Sancar's research has provided critical insights into how cells maintain genomic integrity and prevent mutations that can lead to cancer and other diseases.

In addition to his Nobel Prize, Sancar has received numerous awards and honors. He is a member of the National Academy of Sciences and the American Academy of Arts and Sciences. Throughout his career, Sancar has been a passionate advocate for science education and research. He has trained and mentored numerous students and postdoctoral researchers, many of whom have gone on to have successful careers in academia and industry. In recognition of his outstanding contributions to science and his dedication to advancing our understanding of DNA repair, Aziz Sancar remains one of the most respected and influential figures in the field of molecular biology and biochemistry.

CHAPTER THIRTY-THREE

FRANCIS CRICK

Francis Crick was born on June 8, 1916, in Northampton, England. He was a pioneering molecular biologist and neuroscientist who is best known for his co-discovery along with James Watson, the double helix structure of DNA. Their pioneering finding which was made public in 1953, completely changed the field of biology and set the stage for our current knowledge of genetics. Significant understandings on the structure of DNA and the storage and transmission of genetic information in living things have been made possible by Crick's work. His discovery of the double helix opened the door for more study into the mechanics behind heredity and evolution while also revealing the wonderful simplicity of the genetic code. Along with Maurice Wilkins and James Watson, he shared the 1962 Nobel Prize in Physiology or Medicine.

Crick made important advances in our understanding of the brain and consciousness in addition to his work on DNA. The fundamental theory of molecular biology, which explains how genetic information moves from DNA to RNA to protein was established by his work. The spirit of scientific inquiry is best represented by Crick's multidisciplinary approach and his ability to face challenging issues with rigor and originality. His contributions to biology have been significant and long-lasting and his reputation as one of the greatest scientists of the 20th century continues to motivate scientists and academics worldwide.

JAMES WATSON

James Watson was born on April 6, 1928, in Chicago, Illinois. He was a pioneering molecular biologist who along with Francis Crick, made one of the most significant discoveries in the history of science, the double helix structure of DNA. Their revolutionary work which was published in 1953, transformed the discipline of biology and gave rise to a basic understanding of the molecular foundation of heredity. The foundation for the modern age of molecular biology was established by Watson and Crick's discovery of the DNA structure. Their findings opened the door to many advancements in biotechnology, agriculture and medicine by disclosing the wonderful simplicity of the genetic code and unlocking the mysteries of heredity.

Watson made important contributions to the fields of genetics and molecular biology in addition to his work on DNA. He has been a prominent person in the field of genomics for many years. He was involved in the Human Genome Project, which attempted to map and sequence the whole human genome. Watson has received a great deal of gratitude and admiration for his multidisciplinary approach to science, his inspirational leadership and his readiness to challenge accepted knowledge. Along James

Crick and Maurice Wilkins, he shared the 1962 Nobel Prize in Physiology or Medicine for their discovery of the molecular structure of DNA. The life work of James Watson, a revolutionary scientist and champion of scientific inquiry inspires and impacts academics and researchers globally.

CHAPTER THIRTY-FIVE

Srinivasa Ramanujan

Srinivasa Ramanujan was born on December 22, 1887, in Erode, India. He was a self-taught mathematical prodigy whose extraordinary contributions to number theory, mathematical analysis and infinite series continue to inspire mathematicians to this day. Ramanujan never had a formal education in mathematics but his natural aptitude and intuitive understanding of the subject allowed him to make important discoveries that shaped the discipline. Ramanujan was known for his elegant, unique and profound work. Mathematicians from all around the world are still doing research on the wealth of mathematical concepts found in his notebooks which are crammed with thousands of theorems and equations. Among his most well known contributions are the partition function, modular forms and mock theta functions.

Ramanujan caught the attention of famous mathematician G. H. Hardy in 1913. Hardy saw the young Indian's genius and extended an invitation for him to study at the University of Cambridge in England. Ramanujan worked with Hardy and other mathematicians at Cambridge where he produced ground-breaking findings in number theory and analysis. Throughout his life, Ramanujan had many difficulties and health problems, yet his enthusiasm for mathematics remained unwavering. He is still regarded as a legendary person in the history of mathematics because of the extraordinary abilities that brought him recognition. Mathematicians and fans both are still captivated and inspired by Srinivasa Ramanujan as one of the greatest mathematical intellect of all time.

CHAPTER THIRTY-SIX

THOMAS ALVA EDISON

Thomas Alva Edison was born on February 11, 1847, in Milan, Ohio. He was one of the most prolific inventors in history, holding over 1,000 patents for his inventions. His inventions and technological advances changed the course of history and established the groundwork for several contemporary enterprises. The invention of the first widely used incandescent light bulb he patented in 1879 for which Edison is most famous. By offering a dependable and effective source of artificial light, this innovation completely changed how people lived and worked transforming evening activities and promoting economic growth.

Edison made important contributions to the invention of the phonograph, motion picture camera and alkaline storage battery. By establishing the Edison Electric Light Company (later General Electric) to commercialize his inventions, he also had a significant impact on the development of the electric power sector. Edison's approach to innovation had been defined by his willingness to fail and his unwavering experimentation. "I have not failed," he famously declared. I have discovered 10,000 ineffective methods." Even today, innovators and business owners are motivated by his willingness to try new things and his perseverance in solving real world issues. The modern world is still being influenced by the inventions and enterprises of Thomas Alva Edison. His innovations have had a significant influence on virtually every aspect of our lives and his creativity and resilience have served as an inspiration to subsequent generations of innovators.

CHAPTER THIRTY-SEVEN

ALEXANDER FLEMING

Alexander Fleming was born on August 6, 1881, in Lochfield, Scotland. He was a pioneering bacteriologist whose accidental discovery of penicillin revolutionized medicine and saved millions of lives. Fleming's research changed the way in which bacterial infections are treated and set the stage for the discovery of antibiotics. In 1928, Fleming discovered that a mold known as Penicillium notatum had infected one of his culture plates and prevented the growth of the Staphylococcus bacterium he was studying at St. Mary's Hospital in London. He made the accidental discovery that penicillin, the first antibiotic possesses antibacterial properties.

Fleming's discovery of penicillin was a significant event in the history of medicine. Many lives were saved by penicillin during and after World War II as it demonstrated remarkable efficacy against a variety of bacterial illnesses such as pneumonia, syphilis and streptococcal infections. Fleming made important advances in bacteriology and immunology in addition to his work on penicillin. Along with Ernst Boris Chain and Howard Florey, he shared the Nobel Prize in 1945 in Physiology or Medicine for discovering penicillin and its potential therapeutic value. Fleming's legacy as a pioneering scientist and medical innovator continues to inspire researchers and medical professionals to explore new avenues for combating infectious diseases. His accidental discovery of penicillin remains one of the most important milestones in the history of medicine demonstrating the power of scientific curiosity and the potential for coincidence to change the course of human history.

CHAPTER THIRTY-EIGHT

GREGOR JOHANN MENDEL

Gregor Johann Mendel was born on July 20, 1822, in Hyncice, Moravia (now Czech Republic). He was a pioneering scientist and Augustinian friar who laid the foundation for the modern science of genetics. He discovered the fundamental rules of inheritance and the fundamental principles of heredity with pea plants in the middle of the 19th century. The traditional beliefs of inheritance in which children inherited a combination of traits from their parents. Mendel proved that traits are inherited in distinct units which we now refer to as genes. He proposed the concept of dominant and recessive alleles and formulated the principles of segregation and independent assortment which describe how these genetic factors are passed from one generation to the next.

Even though Mendel's revolutionary findings were ignored while he was alive, subsequent scientists like Hugo de Vries, Carl Correns and Erich von Tschermak rediscovered and valued his work. Mendel's laws of inheritance served as a theoretical foundation for the study of heredity in all living things and established the science of genetics. As the founder of modern genetics, Gregor Johann Mendel continues to be honored today. His pioneering research and creative techniques revolutionized the field of heredity and opened the door of modern genetics, its advancements and applications in biology, agriculture and medicine.

CHAPTER THIRTY-NINE

BARBARA MCCLINTOCK

Barbara McClintock was born on June 16, 1902, in Hartford, Connecticut. She was a pioneering geneticist whose discoveries revolutionized our understanding of the structure and function of chromosomes. She is best known for her work on transposable elements or "jumping genes" which revealed the dynamic nature of the genome and challenged prevailing notions of genetic stability. McClintock primarily conducted her research with maize (corn) plants and demonstrated that certain genetic elements have the ability to move within the genome changing their position and affecting gene expression. This discovery provided crucial insights into the mechanisms of genetic regulation and inheritance.

Despite facing skepticism and resistance from the scientific community, McClintock persisted in her research and continued to make significant discoveries throughout her career. In 1983, she was awarded the Nobel Prize in Physiology or Medicine for her work on transposable elements and becoming the first and only woman to receive an unshared Nobel

Prize in that category. McClintock's work has had a lasting impact on the field of genetics influencing research in molecular biology, developmental biology and evolutionary biology. Her innovative approach to science, keen observational skills and willingness to challenge conventional wisdom continue to inspire scientists and scholars to explore the mysteries of the genome.

CHAPTER FORTY

ERNEST RUTHERFORD

Ernest Rutherford was born on August 30, 1871, in Brightwater, New Zealand. He was a pioneering physicist who made significant discoveries in the field of nuclear physics. He is best known for his investigations into the structure of the atom and his pioneering work on radioactivity for which he was also known as the "father of nuclear physics." Rutherford's most famous experiment was conducted in 1909 involved bombarding a thin gold foil with alpha particles. Surprisingly, some of the alpha particles were deflected at large angles while others passed straight through the foil. This led Rutherford to propose the nuclear model of the atom in which the atom consists mostly of empty space with a dense positively charged nucleus at its center. In addition to his work on atomic structure, Rutherford made significant contributions to the study of radioactivity and nuclear reactions. He discovered the concept of radioactive half-life, developed the first artificial nuclear reaction and was the first to artificially split the atom. In 1908, he was awarded the Nobel Prize in Chemistry for his investigations into the disintegration of the elements and the chemistry of radioactive substances. He was the first Oceanian Nobel laureate and the first to perform the awarded work in Canada.

Rutherford's significant discoveries laid the foundation for many subsequent developments in nuclear physics and chemistry including the development of atomic bomb and in the field of nuclear medicine. Ernest Rutherford's pioneering works in nuclear physics continues to inspire generations of physicists and researchers to explore the mysteries of the atomic nucleus.

CHAPTER FORTY-ONE

JONAS SALK

Jonas Salk was born on October 28, 1914, in New York City. He was a pioneering medical researcher who developed the first successful polio vaccine which saved countless lives and changed the course of medical history. His work on the polio vaccine marked one of the greatest achievements in modern medicine and remains a foundation work to combat against infectious diseases. In the early 1950s, polio was a dreaded disease that caused paralysis and death particularly among children. Salk dedicated himself to finding a safe and effective vaccine to prevent polio infection. In 1955, after years of research and testing, Salk and his team successfully developed an inactivated polio vaccine (IPV) that was proven to be safe and effective in preventing polio.

The introduction of the Salk vaccine dramatically reduced the incidence of polio in the United States and around the world leading to the eventual eradication of the disease in many countries. Salk's vaccine was hailed as a medical breakthrough and made him a national hero. In addition to his work on the polio vaccine, Salk also made significant contributions to the fields of virology, immunology and public health. He founded the Salk Institute for Biological Studies in La Jolla, California, which remains a leading center for biomedical research and education. Jonas Salk's dedication to scientific inquiry, his commitment to public health and his humanitarian efforts have had a lasting impact on the world. His pioneering work in the field of medical science continues to inspire researchers and public health professionals to strive for a healthier world.

CHAPTER FORTY-TWO

LISE MEITNER

Lise Meitner was born on November 7, 1878, in Vienna, Austria-Hungary (now Austria). She was a pioneering physicist who made groundbreaking contributions to the field of nuclear physics. Despite facing discrimination as a woman in the male-dominated scientific community, Meitner's intellect and perseverance led her to become one of the most respected scientists of her time. Meitner's most significant contribution came in collaboration with Otto Hahn, with whom she discovered nuclear fission in 1938. Their experiments demonstrated that bombarding uranium atoms with neutrons could split the nucleus into smaller fragments releasing a tremendous amount of energy. This discovery laid the groundwork for the development of nuclear reactors and atomic bombs and had far reaching implications for both science and society.

Despite her integral role in the discovery of nuclear fission, Meitner's contributions were often overlooked and she was not awarded the Nobel Prize in Chemistry that was given solely to Hahn in 1944. However, Meitner's legacy as a pioneering scientist and advocate for women in science continues to be celebrated today. She was a trailblazer who defied societal expectations and paved the way for future generations of female scientists to pursue their passions and make their mark on the world of science. Lise Meitner's contributions to nuclear physics and her enduring legacy as a role model for women in STEM fields continue to inspire scientists and educators around the world.

CHAPTER FORTY-THREE

CARL LINNAEUS

Carl Linnaeus was born on May 23, 1707, in Råshult, Sweden. He was a pioneering botanist, zoologist and taxonomist who is often regarded as the father of modern taxonomy. Linnaeus' systematic approach to classifying and naming organisms revolutionized the field of biology and laid the foundation for the modern system of binomial nomenclature. Linnaeus's most significant contribution was the development of the Linnaean system of classification which introduced a hierarchical structure for organizing and categorizing living organisms based on their shared characteristics. His system which classified organisms into hierarchical groups such as kingdom, phylum, class, order, family, genus and species provided a standardized framework for the study of biodiversity and laid the groundwork for the modern classification of plants and animals.

In addition to his work on taxonomy, Linnaeus made significant contributions to the study of botany and zoology. He authored numerous works on plant and animal species including the landmark publication "Systema Naturae" which outlined his taxonomic system and provided a comprehensive overview of the known biodiversity of his time. Linnaeus's contributions to science had a profound and lasting impact on the field of biology. His systematic approach to classification and his emphasis on standardized naming conventions continue to be used by biologists around the world to this day. Carl Linnaeus's legacy as a pioneering scientist and taxonomist continues to be celebrated for its profound influence on our understanding of the natural world.

IBN AL HAYTHAM

Ibn al Haytham was born in 965 AD in Basra, Iraq. He was a pioneering scientist, mathematician, astronomer and philosopher who made significant contributions to various fields of knowledge particularly in optics and the scientific method. Often referred to as the "father of modern optics," Ibn al Haytham's work laid the foundation for the scientific understanding of light and vision. One of Ibn al Haytham's most famous works is his monumental treatise "Kitab al Manazir" (Book of Optics), where he outlined his theories on optics, vision and light. In this work, he challenged the prevailing theories of vision proposed by the ancient Greeks and introduced the concept of experimentation and empirical observation as the basis for scientific inquiry.

Ibn al Haytham's contributions to optics were groundbreaking. He accurately described the nature of light, proposed the concept of rectilinear propagation of light and explained the process of vision through the formation of images on the retina. His work laid the foundation for the development of the modern scientific understanding of optics and influenced later scientists such as Johannes Kepler, René Descartes and

Isaac Newton. In addition to his work in optics, Ibn al Haytham made significant contributions to mathematics, astronomy and philosophy. His emphasis on empirical observation and systematic experimentation laid the groundwork for the scientific method and helped pave the way for the scientific revolution in Europe centuries later. Ibn al Haytham's legacy as a pioneering scientist and philosopher continues to be celebrated today for his profound contributions to human knowledge and understanding.

CHAPTER FORTY-FIVE

NEIL deGRASSE TYSON

Neil deGrasse Tyson was born on October 5, 1958, in New York City. He is an astrophysicist, science communicator and public intellectual known for his ability to make complex scientific concepts accessible and engaging to the general public. Tyson's passion for science and his talent for communication have made him one of the most prominent figures in the popularization of science in the 21st century. Tyson's career has been marked by a commitment to education and outreach. He has served as the director of the Hayden Planetarium at the American Museum of Natural History in New York City and has been a frequent guest on television programs, podcasts and radio shows where he shares his insights on astronomy, astrophysics and the wonders of the universe.

In addition to his work as a science communicator, Tyson is also a prolific author and researcher. He has written several bestselling books on astrophysics and cosmology including "Death by Black Hole" and "Astrophysics for People in a Hurry" which have helped bring complex scientific concepts to a wide audience. Tyson's influence extends beyond the realm of science education. He has been a vocal advocate for the importance of science literacy, critical thinking and evidence based decision making in society. His engaging and accessible approach to science communication has inspired millions of people around the world to develop a deeper appreciation for the wonders of the universe and the power of scientific inquiry.

CHAPTER FORTY-SIX

HANS GEIGER

Hans Geiger was born on September 30, 1882, in Neustadt an der Haardt, Germany. He was a pioneering physicist best known for his invention of the Geiger counter, a device used to detect and measure ionizing radiation. His work on radiation detection and nuclear physics had a profound impact on scientific research and applications in fields such as medicine, nuclear energy and environmental monitoring. Geiger began his scientific career studying physics at the University of Erlangen and later at the University of Munich, where he earned his doctorate under the supervision of Max Planck. He went on to work with Ernest Rutherford at the University of Manchester where he developed the Geiger Marsden experiment which provided crucial evidence for the existence of the atomic nucleus.

In 1928, Geiger collaborated with Walther Müller to develop the first practical Geiger counter, a device that detects and measures ionizing radiation by counting the number of ionization events it produces. The Geiger counter quickly became an essential tool in radiation detection and has been used in diverse applications from medical imaging to nuclear physics research to monitoring environmental radiation levels. Throughout his career, Geiger made significant contributions to the field of nuclear physics including his work on the Geiger Nuttall law, which describes the relationship between the half life of a radioactive isotope and the energy of the emitted alpha particles. His pioneering research and inventions continue to have a lasting impact on scientific and technological advancements in the field of radiation detection and nuclear science.

CHAPTER FORTY-SEVEN

ROBERT OPPENHEIMER

Robert Oppenheimer was born on April 22, 1904, in New York City. He was a theoretical physicist and one of the key figures in the development of the atomic bomb during World War II. His leadership of the Manhattan Project, the top-secret U.S. government program to develop the atomic bomb, earned him a place in history as one of the most influential scientists of the 20th century. Oppenheimer's early career was marked by groundbreaking research in theoretical physics particularly in the fields of quantum mechanics and nuclear physics. He made significant contributions to our understanding of subatomic particles and the behavior of matter at the atomic level.

During World War II, Oppenheimer was recruited to lead the Manhattan Project where he oversaw the design and construction of the first atomic bombs. His leadership and scientific expertise were instrumental in the successful development of the bomb, which ultimately played a decisive role in ending the war. After the war, Oppenheimer became a vocal advocate for arms control and nuclear disarmament. He spoke out against the use of nuclear weapons and worked to promote international cooperation in the peaceful use of atomic energy. Despite his contributions to science and his efforts to promote peace, Oppenheimer's legacy is complex. He faced scrutiny and controversy during the McCarthy era for his leftist political views and associations and he was eventually stripped of his security clearance in 1954 after being accused of communist sympathies. Regardless of these challenges, Robert Oppenheimer remains one of the most significant figures in the history of science and technology. His contributions to nuclear physics and his role in the development of the atomic bomb have left an indelible mark on the course of human history shaping the modern world in profound ways.

CHAPTER FORTY-EIGHT

Claude Shannon

Claude Shannon was born on April 30, 1916, in Petoskey, Michigan. He was a mathematician, electrical engineer and cryptographer who is often referred to as the "father of information theory." His groundbreaking work laid the foundation for the digital revolution and transformed the fields of communication, cryptography and computer science. Shannon's most influential contribution came in 1948 with the publication of his seminal paper, "A Mathematical Theory of Communication" which introduced the concept of information entropy and laid the groundwork for the mathematical study of communication systems. In this paper, Shannon demonstrated that information could be quantified and transmitted efficiently using binary digits, or bits and established the fundamental principles of coding and data compression.

Shannon's work on information theory had far reaching implications for the development of telecommunications, digital computing and cryptography. His insights into the nature of information and communication laid the foundation for the design of modern communication systems including the Internet and paved the way for the digital revolution that has transformed society in the 20th and 21st centuries. In addition to his work on information theory, Shannon made significant contributions to the fields of cryptography and artificial intelligence. His pioneering work continues to influence research and innovation in communication technology, computer science and mathematics and his legacy as a visionary thinker and trailblazer in information theory remains unparalleled.

CHAPTER FORTY-NINE

JOHN VON NEUMANN

John von Neumann was born on December 28, 1903, in Budapest, Hungary. He was a brilliant mathematician, physicist, computer scientist and polymath. His work laid the foundation for modern computing and significantly influenced the development of game theory, quantum mechanics and the design of digital computers. Von Neumann's most significant contributions came in the field of mathematics and computer science. He made pioneering advancements in the fields of set theory, functional analysis and mathematical logic and he played a key role in the development of the modern digital computer. Von Neumann's work on the architecture of stored program computers, outlined in his seminal paper "First Draft of a Report on the EDVAC" established the basic principles of computer design that are still in use today.

In addition to his work in mathematics and computer science, von Neumann made significant contributions to the fields of physics and economics. He played a key role in the development of quantum mechanics and game theory and his work had a profound impact on the fields of nuclear physics and strategic decision making. Von Neumann's intellect, creativity and versatility made him one of the most influential scientists and thinkers of the 20th century. His legacy continues to inspire researchers and innovators across a wide range of disciplines and his contributions to science and technology have had a lasting impact on the modern world.

CHAPTER FIFTY

ANDRE MARIE AMPERE

Andre Marie Ampere was born on January 20, 1775, in Lyon, France. He was a pioneering physicist and mathematician who made significant contributions to the understanding of electromagnetism and the development of the field of electrodynamics. Ampere's work laid the foundation for modern physics and played a crucial role in the development of technologies such as electric motors, telegraphy, and electrical engineering. Ampere's most significant contribution came with his formulation of Ampere's Law, one of the fundamental equations of electromagnetism. This law describes the relationship between electric currents and the magnetic fields they produce providing a quantitative description of the electromagnetic force.

In addition to his work on electromagnetism, Ampere made important contributions to the understanding of electrical circuits and the mathematical formulation of electromagnetic phenomena. His research laid the groundwork for the development of the concept of the electromagnetic field which revolutionized our understanding of the nature of electricity and magnetism. Ampere's legacy as a pioneering scientist and mathematician continues to be celebrated today. The unit of electric current, the ampere (symbol: A), is named in his honor reflecting his profound contributions to the field of electromagnetism. Andre Marie Ampere's work remains foundational to the study of physics and continues to inspire researchers and engineers in their quest to understand the mysteries of the universe.

CHAPTER FIFTY-ONE

HENRI POINCARE

Henri Poincare was born on April 29, 1854, in Nancy, France. He was a preeminent mathematician, physicist, and philosopher who made profound contributions to a wide range of fields including mathematics, celestial mechanics, topology and the philosophy of science. Poincare's work laid the foundation for many areas of modern mathematics and theoretical physics and had a lasting impact on the development of 20th-century science. Poincare's contributions to mathematics were wide ranging and influential. He made significant advancements in the study of differential equations, algebraic topology and the theory of dynamical systems among other areas. His work on the three body problem in celestial mechanics and the theory of dynamical systems laid the groundwork for chaos theory and the modern study of complex systems.

In addition to his mathematical achievements, Poincare was also a prolific writer and philosopher of science. His philosophical writings explored the nature of scientific knowledge, the role of intuition and creativity in mathematical discovery and the foundations of geometry and physics. Poincare's ideas on the philosophy of science had a profound impact on the development of 20th century philosophy and continue to influence debates in the philosophy of mathematics and physics today.

CHAPTER FIFTY-TWO

GUGLIELMO MARCONI

Guglielmo Marconi was born on April 25, 1874, in Bologna, Italy. He was an Italian inventor, engineer and entrepreneur who is credited with the development of the first successful long distance wireless telegraphy system. Marconi's pioneering work laid the foundation for modern wireless communication and earned him the title of the "father of radio." Marconi's interest in wireless telegraphy began in his youth when he became fascinated by the possibility of sending messages through the air without the need for wires. In 1895, at the age of 21, he successfully transmitted a wireless signal over a distance of one mile marking the beginning of his groundbreaking research in wireless communication. Marconi's most significant achievement came in 1901 when he successfully transmitted the first transatlantic wireless signal spanning a distance of over 2,100 miles from Poldhu, Cornwall, in England to Signal Hill, Newfoundland in Canada. This historic feat revolutionized communication and ushered in the era of global wireless telegraphy.

In addition to his work in wireless communication, Marconi made significant contributions to the development of radio technology including the invention of the Marconi antenna and the development of radio broadcasting. His pioneering work laid the foundation for the development of modern radio and paved the way for the emergence of other wireless technologies such as television and mobile phones. Marconi's contributions to the field of wireless communication earned him numerous honors and accolades including the Nobel Prize in Physics in 1909. His legacy as a pioneer in the field of radio technology continues to be celebrated today and his inventions have had a profound impact on the way we communicate and interact in the modern world.

CHAPTER FIFTY-THREE

PIERRE SIMON LAPLACE

Pierre Simon Laplace was born on March 23, 1749, in Beaumont en Auge, France. He was a French mathematician, physicist and astronomer who made significant contributions to a wide range of scientific disciplines including mathematics, celestial mechanics, probability theory and statistics. Laplace's work laid the foundation for many areas of modern mathematics and physics and had a profound impact on the development of science in the 18th and 19th centuries. Laplace's most famous work is his monumental five volume treatise "Celestial Mechanics," published between 1799 and 1825. In this work, Laplace developed a comprehensive mathematical theory of the motions of celestial bodies including the planets, moons and comets based on Isaac Newton's laws of motion and gravitation. His mathematical models and analytical methods revolutionized the field of celestial mechanics and enabled scientists to accurately predict the movements of celestial bodies with unprecedented precision.

In addition to his work in celestial mechanics, Laplace made significant contributions to the fields of probability theory and statistics. He introduced the concept of Bayesian probability and developed techniques for estimating the parameters of probability distributions from observed data. His work laid the foundation for the modern theory of probability and statistics which had a profound impact on fields such as economics, finance, and biology. Laplace's contributions to science and mathematics earned him numerous honors and accolades including election to the French Academy of Sciences and the Royal Society of London. His legacy as one of the greatest mathematicians and scientists of the Enlightenment continues to be celebrated today and his work remains a cornerstone of modern mathematics and physics.

HIPPOCRATES

Hippocrates was born around 460 BC on the Greek island of Kos, is widely regarded as the "Father of Medicine" and one of the most influential figures in the history of medicine. He is best known for revolutionizing the practice of medicine by establishing it as a distinct field based on rational observation, clinical experience and ethical principles. Hippocrates's most enduring contribution is the Hippocratic Oath, a moral code for physicians that emphasizes the importance of patient care, confidentiality and ethical conduct. This oath, which is still taken by medical graduates today reflects Hippocrates's commitment to the well being of patients and the ethical practice of medicine.

In addition to the Hippocratic Oath, Hippocrates made significant advancements in medical knowledge and practice. He emphasized the importance of careful observation and detailed clinical examination in diagnosing and treating diseases and he rejected supernatural explanations for illness in favor of naturalistic explanations based on the principles of anatomy and physiology. Hippocrates's approach to medicine laid the foundation for the scientific study of disease and the practice of evidence based medicine. His teachings and writings collected in the Hippocratic Corpus have had a profound and lasting impact on the field of medicine and continue to be studied and celebrated by physicians and scholars around the world. Hippocrates's legacy as a pioneer of rational medicine and medical ethics remains as relevant today as it was over two millennia ago.

CHAPTER FIFTY-FIVE

TYCHO BRAHE

Tycho Brahe was born on December 14, 1546, in Knudstrup, Denmark. He was a Danish nobleman, astronomer and alchemist who made significant contributions to the fields of astronomy and observational science. Brahe's meticulous observations of the night sky laid the groundwork for the modern understanding of planetary motion and helped pave the way for the development of Kepler's laws of planetary motion. Brahe's most famous accomplishment was his extensive collection of astronomical observations which he meticulously recorded over several decades using state of the art instruments of his own design. His observations were some of the most accurate and detailed of his time and they provided crucial data for later astronomers including Johannes Kepler and Isaac Newton.

In addition to his observational work, Brahe proposed a new model of the universe known as the Tychonic system which combined elements of the geocentric and heliocentric models. In this system, the Earth remained stationary at the center of the universe while the sun and moon orbited around it and the other planets orbited around the sun. Although the Tychonic system was eventually superseded by the heliocentric model proposed by Copernicus and later refined by Kepler and Newton, Brahe's contributions to observational astronomy and the study of planetary motion remain invaluable to this day. Brahe's legacy as a pioneering astronomer and observational scientist continues to be celebrated today. His meticulous observations and innovative methods laid the foundation for modern astronomy and helped to shape our understanding of the cosmos.

CHAPTER FIFTY-SIX

JOSEPH PRIESTLEY

Joseph Priestley (1733-1804) was Born in England. He was a polymath whose diverse contributions left an indelible mark on science, religion and society. Priestley's insatiable curiosity led him to explore various fields including chemistry, theology and political philosophy. His most notable achievement was the discovery of oxygen in 1774, a pivotal moment in the history of science that revolutionized our understanding of combustion and respiration. This groundbreaking work laid the foundation for modern chemistry and earned him a place among the great scientific minds of his time.

Beyond his scientific endeavors, Priestley was also a prominent figure in the intellectual landscape of the 18th century. A staunch advocate of liberal and radical causes, he championed religious tolerance, social reform and the rights of the individual. His writings on politics and theology including "The Rights of Man" and "The Corruptions of Christianity" sparked controversy and influenced the thinking of his contemporaries. Despite facing criticism and persecution for his radical beliefs, Priestley remained steadfast in his convictions believing fervently in the power of reason and enlightenment to bring about positive change in society. His legacy continues to inspire scientists, philosophers and activists alike reminding us of the transformative potential of knowledge and the pursuit of truth.

CHAPTER FIFTY-SEVEN

JOHN DALTON

John Dalton (1766–1844) was an English chemist, physicist and meteorologist whose pioneering work laid the foundation for modern atomic theory. Born into modest beginnings in Cumberland, England. Dalton overcame numerous obstacles to become one of the most influential scientists of his time. Dalton's most significant contribution came in 1803 with the publication of his atomic theory which proposed that all matter is composed of indivisible particles called atoms. He further posited that atoms of different elements have different weights and combine in simple, whole number ratios to form compounds. This theory revolutionized the field of chemistry providing a framework for understanding chemical reactions and the composition of matter.

In addition to his work on atomic theory, Dalton made significant contributions to the study of gases developing the concept of partial pressures and formulating Dalton's law of partial pressures. Dalton's meticulous approach to scientific inquiry and his commitment to empirical evidence set a standard for future generations of scientists. His legacy continues to resonate in the principles of modern chemistry and physics underscoring the importance of observation, experimentation and theoretical rigor in the pursuit of scientific knowledge. Dalton's life and work stand as a testament to the power of curiosity and perseverance in the face of adversity.

114

CHAPTER FIFTY-EIGHT

ENRICO FERMI

Enrico Fermi (1901–1954) was born in Rome, Italy. He was physicist renowned for his contributions to theoretical and experimental physics, particularly in the fields of nuclear and particle physics. Fermi displayed an exceptional aptitude for mathematics and science from a young age. Fermi's early research focused on statistical mechanics and quantum theory, laying the foundation for his later groundbreaking work in nuclear physics. In 1934, he achieved international acclaim with his discovery of the phenomenon of slow neutrons which paved the way for the discovery of nuclear fission. This discovery was instrumental in the development of atomic energy and the eventual creation of the atomic bomb. During World War II, Fermi played a pivotal role in the Manhattan Project leading a team of scientists in the construction of the world's first nuclear reactor known as the Chicago Pile-1. His contributions to the project were instrumental in the successful development of the atomic bomb.

After the war, Fermi continued to make significant contributions to physics including his work on beta decay and the development of the theory of weak interactions. He was awarded the Nobel Prize in Physics in 1938 for his work on induced radioactivity. Fermi's legacy extends far beyond his scientific achievements, he was also known for his humility, integrity and dedication to teaching and mentorship. His pioneering research and innovative approach to physics continue to inspire scientists and researchers around the world.

CHAPTER FIFTY-NINE

EMMY NOETHER

Emmy Noether (1882–1935) was born in Germany. She was a pioneering mathematician whose groundbreaking work profoundly influenced the fields of abstract algebra and theoretical physics. Noether faced barriers to higher education as a woman but overcame societal obstacles to become one of the most important mathematicians of the 20th century. Noether's most significant contributions lie in the realm of abstract algebra and its applications to theoretical physics. She developed what is now known as Noether's theorem which establishes a fundamental connection between symmetries and conservation laws in physics. This theorem has far-reaching implications in fields such as quantum mechanics, general relativity and particle physics providing a deep understanding of the underlying principles governing the universe.

Despite facing discrimination and exclusion from academic positions due to her gender and Jewish heritage, Noether persevered in her pursuit of mathematical excellence. She found refuge at the University of Göttingen where she collaborated with luminaries such as David Hilbert and Felix

Klein, making significant contributions to the development of modern mathematics. Noether's brilliance and resilience continue to inspire generations of mathematicians and scientists underscoring the importance of diversity and inclusivity in academia. Her legacy serves as a testament to the power of intellect and perseverance in overcoming adversity and advancing human knowledge.

CHAPTER SIXTY

GERTY CORI

Gerty Cori (1896–1957) was born in Prague. She was a pioneering biochemist whose groundbreaking research laid the foundation for our understanding of carbohydrate metabolism. She overcame gender barriers to become the third woman to win a Nobel Prize in science, and the first woman to win the Nobel Prize in Physiology or Medicine. Cori's most notable contributions came in collaboration with her husband Carl Cori, with whom she shared the Nobel Prize. Together they elucidated the biochemical pathways involved in glycogen metabolism particularly the conversion of glycogen to glucose 1 phosphate and vice versa. Their work led to the discovery of the Cori cycle, a crucial physiological process that regulates glucose levels in the body during periods of fasting and exercise.

Despite facing discrimination as a woman in the male dominated field of science, Cori's intellect and perseverance propelled her to the forefront of biochemistry. She was a trailblazer for women in science, breaking down barriers and inspiring future generations of female scientists. Cori's legacy endures not only in her scientific achievements but also in her role as a pioneer for women in STEM fields. Her contributions to our understanding of metabolism continue to impact research in biochemistry and medicine highlighting the importance of diversity and inclusivity in scientific inquiry.

CHAPTER SIXTY-ONE

HAROLD UREY

Harold Urey (1893–1981) was born in Indiana. He was an American chemist whose groundbreaking work in isotopic chemistry earned him the Nobel Prize in Chemistry in 1934. Urey's scientific career was marked by pioneering research across various disciplines including physical chemistry, geochemistry and cosmochemistry. Urey's most notable achievement came with the discovery of deuterium, a heavy isotope of hydrogen in 1931. This discovery revolutionized our understanding of atomic structure and chemical bonding laying the groundwork for the field of isotopic chemistry.

Throughout his career, Urey made significant contributions to our understanding of the Earth's origin and evolution. He proposed the theory of planetary accretion which suggests that planets form through the gradual accumulation of smaller celestial bodies. His work on the isotopic composition of meteorites provided valuable insights into the early history of the solar system. During World War II, Urey played a crucial role in the Manhattan Project contributing to the development of the atomic bomb. After the war, he became an advocate for peaceful uses of nuclear energy and a vocal critic of nuclear weapons testing. Urey's legacy as a scientist and humanitarian endures with his contributions to chemistry and our understanding of the Universe continuing to inspire future generations of researchers.

CHAPTER SIXTY-TWO

GRACE HOPPER

Grace Hopper (1906–1992) was born in New York City. She was a pioneering computer scientist and naval officer whose contributions to the field of computer science revolutionized the way we think about programming and software development. Hopper's early fascination with mathematics and technology paved the way for a remarkable career that spanned over four decades. Hopper's most enduring legacy lies in her work on the development of programming languages and compiler technology. She was instrumental in the creation of the first compiler A 0, which translated mathematical symbols into machine code and laid the foundation for modern programming languages. Her subsequent work on the development of COBOL (Common Business Oriented Language), one of the first high level programming languages revolutionized software development by making it accessible to a broader audience.

In addition to her pioneering work in computer science, Hopper made significant contributions to the United States Navy, where she rose to the rank of rear admiral. She was a trailblazer for women in the military becoming one of the first female admirals in U.S. history. Hopper's innovative spirit, resilience and dedication to advancing technology continue to inspire generations of computer scientists and engineers. Her legacy as a visionary leader in both the fields of technology and military service remains unparalleled, cementing her status as a true pioneer in the history of computing.

CHAPTER SIXTY-THREE

ROBERT GODDARD

Robert Goddard (1882–1945) was born in Worcester, Massachusetts. He was an American physicist and engineer often hailed as the father of modern rocketry. Goddard's fascination with space exploration began at an early age inspired by the science fiction novels of Jules Verne. Goddard's pioneering research laid the groundwork for the development of liquid fueled rockets. In 1926, he successfully launched the world's first liquid fueled rocket marking a monumental achievement in the history of space exploration. This groundbreaking feat demonstrated the practicality of rocket propulsion and paved the way for future advancements in rocket technology.

Throughout his career, Goddard made numerous contributions to the field of rocketry including the invention of the multi stage rocket and the development of gyroscopic control systems. His work laid the foundation for the space age and inspired a new generation of scientists and engineers to pursue the dream of space exploration. Despite facing skepticism and ridicule from his peers, Goddard remained undeterred in his pursuit of scientific discovery. His innovative spirit, perseverance and visionary thinking continue to inspire generations of space enthusiasts and serve as a testament to the power of human ingenuity in unlocking the mysteries of the universe.

CHAPTER SIXTY-FOUR

JAMES CHADWICK

James Chadwick (1891–1974) was born in England. He was a British physicist renowned for his discovery of the neutron, a sub atomic particle with no electric charge, in 1932. Chadwick's groundbreaking research revolutionized the field of nuclear physics and earned him the Nobel Prize in Physics in 1935. Chadwick's discovery of the neutron was a pivotal moment in the history of science providing key insights into the structure of the atomic nucleus and the nature of nuclear forces. His experiments demonstrated that the nucleus of an atom contains not only positively charged protons but also electrically neutral neutrons, which play a crucial role in stabilizing the nucleus.

Chadwick's work laid the foundation for the development of nuclear energy and the atomic bomb, making significant contributions to both scientific understanding and practical applications. During World War II, he played a vital role in the British atomic weapons program contributing to the allied efforts to harness the power of nuclear fission. Throughout his career, Chadwick was known for his meticulous experimental technique and his dedication to advancing our understanding of the fundamental forces of nature. His legacy as a pioneering physicist continues to inspire scientists and researchers around the world underscoring the importance of curiosity, perseverance and rigorous scientific inquiry.

CHAPTER SIXTY-FIVE

CLYDE TOMBAUGH

Clyde Tombaugh (1906–1997) was born on a farm in Illinois. He was an American astronomer best known for his discovery of Pluto, the ninth planet in our solar system at the time, in 1930. Tombaugh developed a passion for astronomy from a young age, building his own telescopes and conducting observations of the night sky. Tombaugh's discovery of Pluto came after years of meticulous observation and analysis at the Lowell Observatory in Arizona. Using a blink comparator, he meticulously compared photographic plates taken at different times, searching for any objects that appeared to move against the backdrop of fixed stars. It was through this painstaking process that Tombaugh identified Pluto as a faint point of light shifting position over time.

The discovery of Pluto captured the public's imagination and solidified Tombaugh's place in astronomical history. However, in 2006, Pluto was reclassified as a "dwarf planet" by the International Astronomical Union, prompting some debate about its status. Beyond his discovery of Pluto, Tombaugh made significant contributions to the study of asteroids and comets, discovering hundreds of these celestial objects over the course of his career. He remained dedicated to astronomy throughout his life inspiring future generations of astronomers with his passion for exploring the mysteries of the universe.

HANS BETHE

Hans Bethe (1906–2005) was born in Strasbourg, then part of Germany. He was a German American physicist whose contributions to theoretical physics and nuclear astrophysics earned him the Nobel Prize in Physics in 1967. Bethe's prolific career spanned several decades and encompassed a wide range of topics from nuclear physics to astrophysics. Bethe's most notable achievement came in the 1930s when he made significant contributions to the theory of nuclear reactions particularly the process of nuclear fusion that powers the Sun and other stars. His groundbreaking work on the carbon nitrogen oxygen (CNO) cycle, a key nuclear reaction pathway in stellar interiors, revolutionized our understanding of stellar energy production.

During World War II, Bethe played a crucial role in the Manhattan Project, the U.S. government's top secret effort to develop the atomic bomb. He led the theoretical division at Los Alamos National Laboratory where he made important contributions to the development of the bomb's design. After the war, Bethe continued to make significant contributions to theoretical physics including his work on the theory of nuclear matter and his research on astrophysical phenomena such as supernovae and neutron stars. Throughout his career, Bethe was known for his exceptional mathematical prowess, his rigorous approach to scientific inquiry and his dedication to mentoring the next generation of physicists. His legacy as a towering figure in 20th century physics continues to inspire scientists around the world.

CHAPTER SIXTY-SEVEN

CHANDRASEKHARA VENKATA RAMAN

Chandrasekhara Venkata Raman (1888–1970), commonly known as C.V. Raman was born in Tiruchirappalli, India. He was an physicist whose groundbreaking work in the field of light scattering earned him the Nobel Prize in Physics in 1930. Raman's fascination with science and mathematics led him to pursue a career in physics. Raman's most significant achievement came in 1928 when he discovered the phenomenon that bears his name, now known as Raman scattering. This discovery demonstrated that when light interacts with matter, some of the scattered light undergoes a change in wavelength providing valuable insights into the molecular structure of materials. Raman scattering has since become an invaluable tool in various scientific disciplines including chemistry, biology and materials science.

In addition to his groundbreaking research, Raman was also a dedicated educator and institution builder. He served as the director of the Indian Institute of Science in Bangalore and played a key role in the establishment of several scientific research institutions in India. Raman's legacy as a pioneering scientist and institution builder continues to inspire generations of researchers in India and around the world. His contributions to our understanding of light and matter have had a profound impact on scientific inquiry and technological innovation, cementing his status as one of the greatest physicists of the 20th century.

CHAPTER SIXTY-EIGHT

ABDUS SALAM

Abdus Salam (1926–1996) was born in British India (now Pakistan). He was a theoretical physicist who made significant contributions to the field of particle physics and was awarded the Nobel Prize in Physics in 1979. Salam's brilliance in mathematics and physics was evident from a young age. Salam's most notable achievement came in collaboration with Sheldon Glashow and Steven Weinberg when they proposed the electroweak theory, which unified the electromagnetic and weak nuclear forces into a single theoretical framework. This theory laid the foundation for the Standard Model of particle physics providing a unified description of three of the four fundamental forces of nature.

In addition to his groundbreaking work in particle physics, Salam was a staunch advocate for science and education in the developing world. He played a key role in the establishment of the International Centre for Theoretical Physics (ICTP) in Trieste, Italy, which provides research and training opportunities for scientists from developing countries. Despite facing various challenges, Salam remained dedicated to advancing scientific knowledge and promoting international collaboration. His contributions to theoretical physics and his advocacy for science education have had a lasting impact inspiring generations of scientists in Pakistan and beyond.

CHAPTER SIXTY-NINE

HAR GOBIND KHORANA

Har Gobind Khorana (1922–2011) was Born in Raipur, a village in Multan, Punjab, British India. An Indian American biochemist whose pioneering research in the field of genetics earned him the Nobel Prize in Physiology or Medicine in 1968. Khorana's early life was marked by a passion for science and a determination to overcome the limitations of his humble beginnings.Khorana's most significant achievement came in the 1960s when he deciphered the genetic code and demonstrated how the nucleotide sequence of nucleic acids determines the amino acid sequence of proteins. His groundbreaking experiments laid the foundation for our current understanding of the genetic code and paved the way for advancements in molecular biology and biotechnology.

In addition to his work on the genetic code, Khorana made significant contributions to our understanding of DNA synthesis and the mechanisms of protein synthesis. His research had far reaching implications for fields such as medicine, agriculture and biotechnology revolutionizing our ability to manipulate and understand the building blocks of life. Throughout his career, Khorana was recognized for his intellect, creativity and dedication to scientific inquiry. His legacy as a pioneering biochemist and geneticist continues to inspire scientists around the world, underscoring the importance of curiosity, perseverance and interdisciplinary collaboration in the pursuit of scientific knowledge.

CHAPTER SEVENTY

VENKATRAMAN RAMAKRISHNAN

Venkatraman Ramakrishnan born in the year of 1952 in Chidambaram, India. He is an Indian American structural biologist who was awarded the Nobel Prize in Chemistry in 2009 for his groundbreaking work on the structure and function of the ribosome. Ramakrishnan's early fascination with science led him to pursue a career in chemistry and biology. Ramakrishnan's most significant contribution came in the early 2000s when he and his colleagues determined the high resolution structure of the ribosome, a molecular machine responsible for protein synthesis in cells. Their research provided unprecedented insights into the molecular mechanisms underlying protein synthesis and paved the way for the development of new antibiotics and therapeutic strategies.

In addition to his Nobel Prize winning research, Ramakrishnan has made significant contributions to our understanding of RNA structure and function. He has also been a vocal advocate for scientific education and research funding, emphasizing the importance of basic research in driving scientific innovation and discovery. Ramakrishnan's legacy as a pioneering structural biologist continues to inspire scientists around the world, highlighting the power of interdisciplinary collaboration and the pursuit of knowledge in advancing our understanding of the biological world.

CHAPTER SEVENTY-ONE

SUBRAHMANYAN CHANDRASEKHAR

Subrahmanyan Chandrasekhar (1910–1995) was born in Lahore, British India (now Pakistan). He was an Indian American astrophysicist whose groundbreaking work in theoretical physics and astrophysics earned him the Nobel Prize in Physics in 1983. Chandrasekhar's early fascination with the stars and the mysteries of the universe propelled him to pursue a career in astronomy. Chandrasekhar's most significant contribution came in the 1930s when he formulated the Chandrasekhar limit, which describes the maximum mass of a stable white dwarf star supported by electron degeneracy pressure. This limit is a fundamental concept in astrophysics and has profound implications for our understanding of stellar evolution, supernovae and black holes.

Despite facing skepticism and resistance from established scientists, Chandrasekhar remained steadfast in his pursuit of scientific truth. His pioneering research on stellar structure and dynamics laid the foundation for modern astrophysics and revolutionized our understanding of the cosmos. In addition to his work on stellar structure, Chandrasekhar made significant contributions to other areas of theoretical physics including fluid dynamics, radiative transfer and general relativity. His intellect, creativity and dedication to scientific inquiry continue to inspire generations of scientists and researchers, underscoring the importance of curiosity, perseverance and rigorous scientific inquiry in unlocking the secrets of the universe.

CHAPTER SEVENTY-TWO

ALFRED NOBEL

Alfred Nobel (1833–1896) was born in Stockholm, Sweden. He was a Swedish inventor, engineer and industrialist best known for inventing dynamite. Nobel's early life was marked by a deep interest in science and technology which he inherited from his father, who was a successful inventor and engineer. Nobel's most famous invention was dynamite, which revolutionized the construction and mining industries, making him a wealthy man. However, he was deeply troubled by the destructive potential of his invention and its use in warfare. In an effort to leave a more positive legacy, Nobel established the Nobel Prizes in his will. These prestigious awards, which recognize outstanding achievements in various fields such as physics, chemistry, medicine, literature, and peace, were intended to honor those who have made significant contributions to humanity.

Nobel's vision for the Nobel Prizes was realized after his death and today, the Nobel Prizes are among the most prestigious awards in the world, celebrating the best and brightest minds in science, literature and peace activism and also in economics. Alfred Nobel's legacy as a visionary inventor and philanthropist continues to inspire generations of scientists, writers and peace activists around the world. His commitment to recognizing excellence and promoting human progress through the Nobel Prizes serves as a testament to the power of innovation and compassion in shaping a better world.

CHAPTER SEVENTY-THREE

HOMI JEHANGIR BHABHA

Homi Jehangir Bhabha (1909–1966) was born into a wealthy and influential Parsi family in Mumbai. He was an Indian nuclear physicist who played a pivotal role in the development of nuclear science and technology in India. Bhabha showed an early aptitude for mathematics and science, which led him to pursue a career in physics. Bhabha's most notable contribution came in the 1940s and 1950s when he laid the groundwork for India's nuclear program. He was instrumental in establishing the Tata Institute of Fundamental Research (TIFR) in Mumbai, which became a hub for cutting edge research in nuclear physics and other scientific disciplines.

In addition to his work on nuclear physics, Bhabha was a visionary leader who played a key role in shaping India's scientific and educational institutions. He served as the first chairman of the Indian Atomic Energy Commission and played a central role in the establishment of the Atomic Energy Establishment, Trombay (AEET), which later became the Bhabha Atomic Research Centre (BARC). Bhabha's legacy as a pioneering scientist and institution builder continues to inspire scientists and policymakers in India and around the world. His contributions to nuclear science and technology laid the foundation for India's emergence as a major player in the global nuclear arena.

CHAPTER SEVENTY-FOUR

WILLIAM HARVEY

William Harvey (1578–1657) was born in Folkestone, England. He was an English physician whose groundbreaking work in anatomy and physiology revolutionized our understanding of the circulatory system. Harvey's early education in medicine laid the foundation for his illustrious career in the medical field. Harvey's most significant contribution came in 1628 with the publication of his seminal work, "De Motu Cordis" ("On the Motion of the Heart"). In this landmark treatise, Harvey presented compelling evidence for the circulation of blood throughout the body, challenging the prevailing theories of his time. He meticulously described the role of the heart as a pump that propels blood through the arteries and veins, providing nutrients and oxygen to the body's tissues and organs.

Harvey's revolutionary insights into the circulatory system transformed the practice of medicine and laid the foundation for modern physiology and cardiovascular medicine. His meticulous observations and rigorous scientific methodology set a standard for future generations of researchers, emphasizing the importance of empirical evidence and careful experimentation in the pursuit of scientific knowledge. Harvey's legacy as a pioneering physician and anatomist endures with his contributions to our understanding of the human body continuing to inspire scientists and medical practitioners around the world.

CHAPTER SEVENTY-FIVE

MEGHNAD SAHA

Meghnad Saha (1893–1956) was born in rural west Bengal. He was an Indian astrophysicist whose pioneering work in the field of thermal ionization and astrophysics earned him international acclaim. Saha's early fascination with mathematics and science led him to pursue a career in physics. Saha's most significant contribution came in the early 1920s when he formulated what is now known as the Saha ionization equation. This equation describes the ionization state of a gas in thermal equilibrium providing valuable insights into the physical conditions of stellar atmospheres and the chemical composition of stars. His work laid the foundation for our understanding of the structure and evolution of stars as well as the formation of elements in the universe.

In addition to his research in astrophysics, Saha made significant contributions to the development of scientific institutions and education in India. He played a key role in the establishment of the Indian Association for the Cultivation of Science (IACS) in Kolkata and served as its director for several years. Saha's legacy as a pioneering astrophysicist and institution builder continues to inspire scientists and researchers in India and around the world. His contributions to our understanding of the cosmos have had a lasting impact on the field of astrophysics highlighting the importance of interdisciplinary collaboration and the pursuit of knowledge in unraveling the mysteries of the universe.

CHAPTER SEVENTY-SIX

SATYENDRA NATH BOSE

Satyendra Nath Bose (1894–1974) was born in Calcutta. He was an Indian physicist whose groundbreaking work laid the foundation for the field of quantum statistics and the Bose-Einstein condensate. Bose's early interest in mathematics and science led him to pursue a career in theoretical physics. Bose's most significant contribution came in 1924 when he derived a new statistical distribution for particles that obeyed quantum principles. This distribution is known as Bose-Einstein statistics, described the behavior of indistinguishable particles, such as photons or atoms in a quantum mechanical system. Bose's work provided a theoretical framework for understanding phenomena such as blackbody radiation and the behavior of gases at low temperatures.

In addition to his work on quantum statistics, Bose made significant contributions to various areas of theoretical physics including the theory of radiation, the theory of the electromagnetic field and the theory of relativity. Despite facing challenges and limited recognition during his lifetime, Bose's contributions to physics have had a profound impact on our understanding of the quantum world. His work laid the foundation for the development of quantum mechanics and inspired generations of physicists to explore the fundamental principles of the universe. Bose's legacy as a pioneering physicist continues to be celebrated in India and around the world.

CHAPTER SEVENTY-SEVEN

DR APJ ABDUL KALAM

Dr APJ Abdul Kalam (1931–2015) was born into a modest family in Rameswaram, Tamil Nadu. He was an eminent Indian scientist, engineer and statesman who served as the 11th President of India from 2002 to 2007. Kalam's journey from a newspaper boy to the highest office in the country is an inspiring testament to the power of hard work, perseverance and dedication to public service. Kalam's contributions to Indian science and technology are unparalleled. He played a pivotal role in the development of India's ballistic missile and nuclear weapons programs, earning him the moniker "Missile Man of India." His leadership and vision propelled India into the league of nations with advanced missile capabilities, bolstering the country's defense and security.

Beyond his scientific achievements, Kalam was a beloved figure known for his humility, integrity and unwavering commitment to youth empowerment and education. He was a passionate advocate for harnessing the potential of India's youth as drivers of progress and social change. Kalam's legacy as a scientist, statesman and mentor continues to inspire millions of people in India and around the world. His vision of a prosperous, technologically advanced and inclusive India lives on, guiding future generations to strive for excellence and contribute to the betterment of society.

CHAPTER SEVENTY-EIGHT

PTOLEMY

Ptolemy (circa 90 AD – circa 168 AD), also known as Claudius Ptolemaeus, was an ancient Greek Egyptian mathematician, astronomer and geographer. He is best known for his geocentric model of the universe, which dominated Western astronomical thought for over a millennium. Ptolemy's most influential work, "Almagest," synthesized the astronomical knowledge of his time and presented a comprehensive mathematical model of the cosmos. In this model, Earth was considered the stationary center of the universe with celestial bodies moving in perfect circles around it. To account for the observed motions of planets and stars, Ptolemy introduced the concept of epicycles- circles upon larger orbits – to explain deviations from uniform circular motion.

Although Ptolemy's model was eventually superseded by the heliocentric model proposed by Copernicus in the 16th century, his contributions to astronomy were significant. His meticulous observations and mathematical techniques laid the groundwork for later astronomers and contributed to the development of trigonometry. In addition to his work in astronomy, Ptolemy made important contributions to geography, producing maps and geographic treatises that remained influential for centuries. Despite the limitations of his geocentric model, Ptolemy's legacy as a pioneering astronomer and geographer endures, underscoring the enduring impact of ancient Greek scholarship on Western science and thought.

CHAPTER SEVENTY-NINE

EUCLID

Euclid (circa 300 BC – circa 265 BC) was an ancient Greek mathematician often referred to as the "Father of Geometry." Little is known about his life, but his work, "Elements," became one of the most influential mathematical texts in history. "Elements" is a comprehensive compilation of Euclidean geometry consisting of 13 books covering a wide range of topics including plane geometry, number theory and solid geometry. Euclid's approach to geometry was axiomatic, meaning that he based his theorems and propositions on a set of self evident axioms and postulates.

One of Euclid's most enduring contributions is the systematization of geometry, where he organized geometric concepts into a logical and coherent framework. His rigorous deductive method which involved deriving new results from established principles became the standard for mathematical reasoning for over two millennia. Euclid's work not only advanced the study of mathematics but also had a profound impact on philosophy, science and education. His geometric principles and logical reasoning influenced thinkers throughout history including Isaac Newton and René Descartes and laid the foundation for modern mathematics as we know it today. Euclid's legacy as a pioneer in mathematical thought continues to inspire mathematicians and educators around the world.

CHAPTER EIGHTY

ARCHIMEDES

Archimedes (circa 287 BC – circa 212 BC) was born in the city of Syracuse on the island of Sicily. He was an ancient Greek mathematician, physicist, engineer and inventor who is widely regarded as one of the greatest mathematicians of all time. One of Archimedes' most famous discoveries is his principle of buoyancy, also known as Archimedes' principle. According to this principle, a body immersed in a fluid experiences an upward force equal to the weight of the fluid displaced by the body. This principle is fundamental to the understanding of flotation and the behavior of ships and submarines in water.

Archimedes also made important contributions to the field of geometry, particularly in the area of calculating areas and volumes of geometric shapes. He developed the method of exhaustion, a precursor to integral calculus which he used to calculate the areas of circles, spheres and other curved shapes. In addition to his mathematical achievements, Archimedes was also an accomplished engineer and inventor. He designed innovative machines such as the screw pump and the Archimedes screw which are still used today in various applications including irrigation and wastewater treatment. Archimedes' legacy as a brilliant mathematician, physicist and engineer continues to inspire scientists and engineers around the world.

160

CHAPTER EIGHTY-ONE

PAUL ERDOS

Paul Erdos (1913–1996) was a Hungarian mathematician known for his prolific output and collaborative approach to mathematics. Born in Budapest, Erdős displayed exceptional mathematical talent from an early age, publishing his first paper at the age of 17. Erdős's most remarkable trait was his collaborative spirit and he is famously remembered for his collaborations with hundreds of mathematicians worldwide. He would often refer to his collaborators as "coauthors" and would travel extensively, staying with colleagues and working together on mathematical problems. This unique approach earned him the nickname "The Man Who Loved Only Numbers."

Erdos made significant contributions to a wide range of mathematical fields including number theory, combinatorics and graph theory. He published over 1,500 mathematical papers in his lifetime, making him one of the most prolific mathematicians in history. In addition to his research, Erdős was known for his eccentric personality and his devotion to mathematics. He eschewed material possessions and lived a frugal lifestyle, devoting himself entirely to the pursuit of mathematical truth. Erdos's legacy as a brilliant mathematician and a beloved figure in the mathematical community lives on, inspiring generations of mathematicians to collaborate, explore and push the boundaries of mathematical knowledge.

CHAPTER EIGHTY-TWO

JOHN BARDEEN

John Bardeen (1908–1991) was born in Madison, Wisconsin. He was an American physicist and electrical engineer who was awarded the Nobel Prize in Physics twice, in 1956 and 1972, making him one of only four individuals to have received the Nobel Prize twice. Bardeen's early interest in science and mathematics led him to pursue a career in physics. Bardeen's first Nobel Prize was awarded for his role in the invention of the transistor, along with Walter Brattain and William Shockley, while working at Bell Labs. The transistor revolutionized the field of electronics, leading to the development of smaller, faster and more reliable electronic devices.

Bardeen's second Nobel Prize was awarded for his theoretical work on superconductivity, a phenomenon where certain materials can conduct electricity with zero resistance at low temperatures. His groundbreaking theory known as the BCS theory (named after Bardeen, Leon Cooper and Robert Schrieffer), provided the first comprehensive explanation of superconductivity and laid the foundation for further research in the field. Throughout his career, Bardeen made numerous other contributions to physics and engineering including research on semiconductors, superfluidity and the theory of solids. His legacy as a pioneering scientist and innovator continues to inspire researchers and engineers in the field of condensed matter physics and electronics.

164

CHAPTER EIGHTY-THREE

CHIEN SHIUNG WU

Chien Shiung Wu (1912–1997) was born in Liuhe, China. She was a Chinese American experimental physicist who made significant contributions to the field of nuclear physics. Wu's early interest in science and mathematics led her to pursue a career in physics. Wu's most notable achievement came during her time at Columbia University where she conducted the Wu Experiment in collaboration with physicists Tsung Dao Lee and Chen Ning Yang. The experiment conducted in 1956 disproved the law of conservation of parity which had been a fundamental principle in particle physics until then. This groundbreaking discovery earned Lee and Yang the Nobel Prize in Physics in 1957, though Wu's pivotal role in designing and conducting the experiment was not recognized by the Nobel Committee.

In addition to her work on parity violation, Wu made significant contributions to the Manhattan Project during World War II where she helped develop the process for separating uranium isotopes for use in the atomic bomb. Throughout her career, Wu faced discrimination and challenges as a woman in the male dominated field of physics. Despite these obstacles, she remained dedicated to her research and advocacy for gender equality in science. Wu's legacy as a pioneering physicist and advocate for diversity and inclusion continues to inspire scientists around the world.

CHAPTER EIGHTY-FOUR

EDWARD OSBORNE WILSON

Edward Osborne Wilson, born in Birmingham, Alabama, in 1929, commonly known as E.O. Wilson, is an American biologist, researcher and naturalist, renowned for his work in ecology, evolutionary biology and conservation. Wilson developed a passion for the natural world at an early age. Wilson's pioneering research has had a profound impact on our understanding of biodiversity and the interconnectedness of ecosystems. His studies on social insects particularly ants, have revealed fundamental principles of social behavior and cooperation in the animal kingdom. Wilson's work on island biogeography provided key insights into the factors influencing species diversity and distribution.

In addition to his scientific contributions, Wilson is a prolific author and advocate for conservation. His books including "The Diversity of Life" and "Biophilia," have inspired generations of readers to appreciate and protect the natural world. Wilson has also been a vocal proponent of environmental education and sustainable development. Throughout his career, Wilson has received numerous awards and honors for his contributions to science and conservation including the Pulitzer Prize for General Nonfiction. His legacy as a pioneering biologist and environmentalist continues to inspire scientists, educators and conservationists around the world.

CHAPTER EIGHTY-FIVE

MURRAY GELL MANN

Murray Gell Mann (1929–2019) was born in New York City. He was an American physicist who made profound contributions to our understanding of the fundamental particles and forces of nature. Gell Mann demonstrated exceptional mathematical talent from a young age, leading him to pursue a career in theoretical physics. Gell Mann's most notable achievement came in 1964 when he proposed the concept of quarks, which are elementary particles that make up protons, neutrons and other hadrons. His quark model revolutionized the field of particle physics providing a framework for understanding the strong nuclear force and the behavior of subatomic particles.

In addition to his work on quarks, Gell Mann made significant contributions to the theory of weak interactions and the development of the "eightfold way," a classification scheme for hadrons based on their symmetrical properties. Gell Mann was awarded the Nobel Prize in Physics in 1969 for his contributions to the classification and symmetries of elementary particles. Throughout his career, he was known for his deep insights, creativity and interdisciplinary approach to scientific inquiry. Gell Mann's legacy as a pioneering physicist continues to influence research in particle physics and beyond. His work laid the foundation for the Standard Model of particle physics which remains the most successful theory to date in describing the fundamental particles and forces of the universe.

CHAPTER EIGHTY-SIX

FRANCIS COLLINS

Francis Collins is an American physician and geneticist known for his leadership in the Human Genome Project and his contributions to genetics and medicine. Born in Virginia in 1950, Collins initially pursued studies in chemistry but later shifted his focus to medicine, earning his M.D. from the University of North Carolina at Chapel Hill. Collins' most significant contribution to science came as the director of the National Human Genome Research Institute (NHGRI) from 1993 to 2008. Under his leadership, the Human Genome Project, an international collaboration to map and sequence the human genome was successfully completed in 2003. This monumental achievement paved the way for groundbreaking discoveries in genetics and medicine revolutionizing our understanding of human biology and disease.

Beyond his work on the Human Genome Project, Collins has made significant contributions to the study of genetic diseases, particularly through his research on cystic fibrosis and other inherited disorders. He has also been a vocal advocate for the ethical and responsible use of genetic information emphasizing the importance of informed consent and privacy protections. In 2009, Collins was appointed as the director of the National Institutes of Health (NIH), where he continues to lead efforts to advance biomedical research and improve public health. His leadership, vision and dedication to scientific inquiry have earned him widespread recognition and respect in the scientific community.

CHAPTER EIGHTY-SEVEN

BENJAMIN FRANKLIN

Benjamin Franklin (1706–1790) was born in Boston, Massachusetts. He was one of the Founding Fathers of the United States and a polymath whose contributions spanned science, politics, diplomacy and literature. Franklin's thirst for knowledge led him to become one of the most influential figures of the American Enlightenment. Franklin's scientific achievements were wide ranging and groundbreaking. He conducted pioneering experiments in electricity, famously demonstrating the nature of lightning through his kite experiment. His work laid the foundation for modern understanding of electricity and earned him international acclaim.

In addition to his scientific pursuits, Franklin was a prominent statesman and diplomat. He played a key role in the American revolution helping to draft the declaration of independence and negotiating crucial alliances with France. His diplomatic efforts were instrumental in securing support for the fledgling United States. Franklin was also a prolific writer and inventor, known for his wit and wisdom. His aphorisms, essays, and almanacs, including "Poor Richard's Almanack," remain popular and influential to this day. Franklin's legacy as a statesman, scientist and intellectual giant continues to inspire generations of Americans and people around the world. His commitment to the pursuit of knowledge, innovation and civic duty exemplifies the values of the American spirit.

CHAPTER EIGHTY-EIGHT

ALEXANDER GRAHAM BELL

Alexander Graham Bell (1847–1922) was born in Edinburgh, Scotland. He was a Scottish born inventor, scientist and engineer who is best known for inventing the telephone. Bell emigrated to Canada and later to the United States where he conducted his most famous work. Bell's fascination with sound and communication led him to experiment with ways to transmit sound over long distances. In 1876, he was awarded the first U.S. patent for the invention of the telephone, a device that revolutionized communication by allowing people to speak to each other over long distances.

In addition to the telephone, Bell made significant contributions to other fields including aviation and education for the deaf. He founded the American Telephone and Telegraph Company (AT&T) which became one of the largest telecommunications companies in the world. Bell's legacy extends far beyond the invention of the telephone. He was a prolific inventor with over 18 patents to his name including inventions in fields such as hydrofoils, metal detectors and optical telecommunications. He was also a prominent advocate for the deaf community, co founding the Volta Bureau which focused on advancing deaf education and research. Bell's pioneering work in telecommunications and his commitment to innovation continue to influence modern technology and communication. He is remembered as one of the most important inventors in history, whose inventions transformed the way people communicate and connect with each other.

CHAPTER EIGHTY-NINE

JOHN SNOW

John Snow (1813–1858) was born in York, England. He was an English physician often regarded as one of the founding figures of modern epidemiology. Snow's pioneering work in the field of public health had a profound impact on our understanding of infectious diseases and their transmission. Snow's most famous achievement came during the 1854 cholera outbreak in London which he meticulously investigated. Through careful mapping of cases and analysis of water sources, Snow demonstrated that the outbreak was caused by contaminated water from a public pump on Broad Street (now Broadwick Street) in Soho. His findings which challenged prevailing miasma theory, ultimately led to the removal of the pump handle, effectively ending the epidemic and revolutionizing the understanding of cholera transmission.

In addition to his work on cholera, Snow made significant contributions to anesthesia and medical hygiene. He is credited with introducing ether as an anesthetic agent and advocating for improved sanitation practices in hospitals. Snow's legacy as a pioneering epidemiologist and public health advocate continues to inspire researchers and practitioners in the field of infectious disease control. His emphasis on evidence based medicine and data driven decision making remains central to the practice of public health today.

CHAPTER NINETY

CHRISTIAAN HUYGENS

Christiaan Huygens (1629–1695) was born into a prominent family in The Hague, Netherlands. He was a Dutch mathematician, physicist and astronomer who made significant contributions to various fields of science during the 17th century. Huygen's displayed exceptional intellectual abilities from a young age. Huygen's most notable achievement came in the field of optics, where he made groundbreaking discoveries about light and vision. He developed the wave theory of light, proposing that light consists of waves propagating through a medium, an idea that laid the foundation for modern wave optics. Huygen's also invented the pendulum clock, a device that greatly improved time keeping accuracy and became widely used across Europe.

In addition to his work in optics and horology, Huygen's made significant contributions to mathematics and astronomy. He discovered Saturn's largest moon, Titan and was the first to propose that Saturn's rings are composed of small individual particles. Huygen's work had a profound impact on the scientific revolution of the 17th century and laid the groundwork for many future discoveries in physics and astronomy. His legacy as a pioneering scientist and polymath continues to be celebrated in the fields of optics, astronomy and horology.

WRIGHT BROTHERS

Orville and Wilbur Wright, commonly known as the Wright Brothers. Born in Dayton, Ohio, Orville (1871–1948) and Wilbur (1867–1912) were two of seven siblings are credited with inventing and building the world's first successful airplane. Their interest in aviation was sparked at an early age influenced by their father's passion for mechanics and their own fascination with the works of famous inventors of the time. In 1896, the Wright Brothers became interested in powered flight after reading about the experiments of German aviator Otto Lilienthal and others. They began their journey by studying the flight of birds and experimenting with kites and gliders. They realized that the key to controlled flight lay in mastering the three axes of motion: roll, pitch and yaw. After years of research and experimentation, the Wright Brothers developed a series of gliders that incorporated a system of wing warping for lateral control. In 1903, they achieved their ultimate goal when they successfully flew the Wright Flyer, a powered airplane at Kitty Hawk, North Carolina. The flight lasted just 12 seconds and covered a distance of 120 feet but it marked the beginning of powered aviation.

Over the following years, the Wright Brothers continued to refine their design and improve the performance of their airplanes. In 1905 they built the Wright Flyer III which was capable of sustained flight and could stay aloft for more than half an hour. The Wright Brothers achievements revolutionized transportation and changed the course of history. Their invention paved the way for the development of modern aviation and opened up new possibilities for travel, commerce and communication. Today, Orville and Wilbur Wright are remembered as pioneers of aviation and their contributions to the field are celebrated around the world.

CHAPTER NINETY-TWO

ROBERT BOYLE

Robert Boyle (1627–1691) was an Anglo Irish natural philosopher, chemist, physicist and inventor who is often regarded as one of the founders of modern chemistry. Born into an aristocratic family in Lismore Castle, Ireland, Boyle's upbringing and education exposed him to the intellectual and scientific advancements of his time. Boyle's most significant contribution to science came with his work on the properties of gases, particularly his formulation of Boyle's law. In 1662, he published "The Sceptical Chymist," a seminal work that challenged traditional alchemical theories and laid the groundwork for modern chemistry. In this book, Boyle introduced the concept of chemical elements and argued for the importance of experimental evidence in scientific inquiry.

In addition to his work in chemistry, Boyle made significant contributions to physics, medicine and natural philosophy. He conducted experiments on the properties of air and the vacuum, investigated the behavior of springs and explored the role of the heart in circulation. Boyle's legacy as a pioneering scientist and thinker continues to be celebrated in the fields of chemistry, physics and philosophy. His emphasis on empirical evidence, skepticism and scientific inquiry laid the foundation for modern scientific method and inspired generations of scientists to explore the mysteries of the natural world.

184

CHAPTER NINETY-THREE

JAMES PRESCOTT JOULE

James Prescott Joule (1818–1889) was born into a wealthy brewing family in Salford, England. He was an English physicist who made significant contributions to the study of thermodynamics and the theory of energy. Joule's interest in science was fostered by his father who encouraged his experiments and investigations. Joule's most famous work came in the field of thermodynamics where he formulated what is now known as the first law of thermodynamics, also known as the law of energy conservation. This principle states that energy cannot be created or destroyed, only transformed from one form to another. Joule's experiments on the relationship between heat and mechanical work played a crucial role in establishing the concept of energy conservation. One of Joule's most famous experiments involved the mechanical equivalent of heat, where he demonstrated the relationship between mechanical energy and heat through the agitation of water. This experiment provided experimental evidence for the concept of energy conservation and laid the foundation for the field of thermodynamics. In honor of James Prescott Joule's contributions to science, the unit of energy in the International System of

Units (SI) is named the joule (J).

In addition to his work on thermodynamics, Joule made significant contributions to the study of electricity and magnetism. He was a pioneer in the development of the electromagnetic theory of light and made important discoveries in the field of electrical conductivity. Joule's legacy as a pioneering physicist continues to be celebrated in the fields of thermodynamics and energy science. His contributions to our understanding of the fundamental principles of energy have had a lasting impact on science and technology.

CHAPTER NINETY-FOUR

PAUL BROCA

Paul Broca (1824–1880) was born in Sainte Foy la Grande, France. He was a French physician, anatomist and anthropologist who made significant contributions to the understanding of the brain and its functions. Broca's early interest in medicine and anatomy led him to pursue a career in the medical field. Broca's most notable contribution came with his discovery of the brain region now known as Broca's area. In 1861, he published a landmark paper describing a patient with a speech impairment caused by damage to a specific area of the brain located in the left frontal lobe. This discovery provided crucial evidence for the localization of speech production in the brain and laid the foundation for the field of neuropsychology.

In addition to his work on Broca's area, Broca made significant contributions to the fields of anthropology and craniometry. He was a pioneer in the study of human evolution and racial anthropology and his research laid the groundwork for modern studies of human variation and diversity. Broca's legacy as a pioneering neuroscientist and anthropologist continues to be celebrated in the fields of medicine, psychology and anthropology. His discoveries have had a lasting impact on our understanding of the brain and its role in language and cognition.

CHAPTER NINETY-FIVE

CHRISTIAAN EIJKMAN

Christiaan Eijkman (1858–1930) was born in the Netherland. He was a Dutch physician and scientist who won the Nobel Prize in Physiology or Medicine in 1929 for his discovery of the cause of beriberi, a nutritional deficiency disease. Eijkman's early medical training led him to work as a military doctor in the Dutch East Indies (now Indonesia), where he made his groundbreaking discovery. Eijkman's research on beriberi began in the late 19th century when he observed that chickens fed on polished rice developed symptoms similar to those of humans suffering from beriberi. He hypothesized that the disease was caused by a dietary deficiency rather than an infectious agent as previously believed. Through further experimentation, Eijkman identified that beriberi was caused by a lack of certain nutrients particularly vitamin B1 (thiamine) present in the outer layers of rice grains that were removed during the polishing process.

Eijkman's discovery of the link between diet and disease laid the foundation for the field of nutrition science and had a profound impact on public health. His work paved the way for the development of methods to prevent and treat nutritional deficiencies ultimately saving countless lives around the world. Eijkman's legacy as a pioneering scientist and humanitarian continues to be celebrated in the field of medicine.

CHAPTER NINETY-SIX

NICOLAUS COPERNICUS

Nicolaus Copernicus (1473–1543) was born in Toruń, Poland. He was a Polish mathematician, astronomer and cleric who revolutionized our understanding of the universe with his heliocentric model of the solar system. Copernicus early interest in mathematics and astronomy led him to pursue a career in these fields. Copernicus most significant contribution to science came with the publication of his seminal work, "De revolutionibus orbium coelestium" ("On the Revolutions of the Celestial Spheres"), in 1543, the year of his death. In this groundbreaking treatise, Copernicus proposed a revolutionary idea that the Earth and other planets revolve around the Sun, rather than the Earth being the center of the universe as previously believed. This heliocentric model challenged the geocentric model that had been dominant for centuries, laid the foundation for modern astronomy and sparked a scientific revolution.

Copernicus heliocentric model was not widely accepted during his lifetime but it paved the way for future astronomers such as Galileo Galilei and Johannes Kepler to further develop and refine our understanding of the cosmos. Copernicus legacy as a pioneering astronomer and thinker continues to be celebrated as one of the most important figures in the history of science.

CHAPTER NINETY-SEVEN

MAX BORN

Max Born (1882–1970) was born in Breslau, Germany (now Wrocław, Poland). He was a German physicist and mathematician who made significant contributions to the fields of quantum mechanics and solid state physics. Born's early work focused on the mathematical foundations of quantum mechanics. Born's most notable contribution came with his formulation of the probabilistic interpretation of the wave function, a cornerstone of quantum mechanics. In 1926, he along with Werner Heisenberg and Pascual Jordan developed the matrix mechanics formulation of quantum mechanics which provided a mathematical framework for describing the behavior of particles at the atomic and subatomic level.

In addition to his work on quantum mechanics, Born made significant contributions to the theory of crystal lattices and the development of solid state physics. His research laid the foundation for our understanding of the electronic structure of crystals and paved the way for the modern field of semiconductor physics. Born's contributions to physics were recognized with the award of the Nobel Prize in Physics in 1954 for his fundamental research in quantum mechanics, especially his statistical interpretation of the wave function. His work continues to be influential in the field of theoretical physics and has had a lasting impact on our understanding of the fundamental principles of the universe.

CHAPTER NINETY-EIGHT

GEORGES LEMAITRE

Georges Lemaitre (1894–1966) was born in Charleroi, Belgium. He was a Belgian Catholic priest, mathematician and physicist who made significant contributions to the field of cosmology. Lemaitre's early education and interest in science led him to pursue studies in mathematics and physics. Lemaitre's most notable contribution came with his proposal of the theory of the expansion of the universe. In 1927, he published a paper suggesting that the universe is expanding, based on his interpretation of the observed red shifts of distant galaxies. Lemaitre's theory which became known as the "primeval atom" or the "Big Bang" theory, proposed that the universe began as a single, infinitely dense point and has been expanding ever since. Lemaitre's groundbreaking idea laid the foundation for modern cosmology and revolutionized our understanding of the origin and evolution of the universe. Despite initial skepticism, his theory gained widespread acceptance and has since been supported by a wealth of observational evidence including the discovery of the cosmic microwave background radiation.

In addition to his work in cosmology, Lemaitre made significant contributions to the fields of mathematics and astrophysics. He was a pioneer in the application of Einstein's theory of general relativity to cosmological models and made important contributions to the development of the expanding universe model. Lemaitre's legacy as a pioneering cosmologist continues to be celebrated in the field of astrophysics. His theory of the Big Bang remains one of the most important and influential ideas in the history of science, shaping our understanding of the universe and our place within it.

CHAPTER NINETY-NINE

EUGENE WIGNER

Eugene Wigner (1902–1995) was born in Budapest, Hungary. He was a Hungarian American theoretical physicist and mathematician who made significant contributions to quantum mechanics, nuclear physics and group theory. Wigner showed exceptional mathematical talent from a young age and his interest in physics led him to pursue a career in theoretical physics. Wigner's most notable contribution came with his development of the theory of symmetries in quantum mechanics particularly his formulation of the Wigner D matrix, which describes the rotational symmetry of quantum mechanical systems. His work on symmetry principles played a crucial role in the development of quantum mechanics and laid the foundation for the application of group theory in physics.

In addition to his work on symmetries, Wigner made important contributions to nuclear physics, including his prediction of the existence of the neutron and his development of the theory of nuclear reactions. He was also instrumental in the development of the atomic bomb during

World War II, serving as a consultant on the Manhattan Project. Wigner was awarded the Nobel Prize in Physics in 1963 for his contributions to the theory of the atomic nucleus and elementary particles, highlighting his significant impact on the field of physics. His work continues to be celebrated for its elegance, depth and profound influence on our understanding of the fundamental laws of nature.

Kalpana Chawla

Kalpana Chawla was born on March 17, 1962, in Karnal, India. She was an extraordinary woman whose achievements and contributions to the field of space exploration continue to inspire people around the world. She developed a passion for flying at a young age. Her dream of reaching the stars led her to pursue a degree in aeronautical engineering from Punjab Engineering College, Chandigarh. Later, she moved to the United States to further her education, earning a Master of Science degree in aerospace engineering from the University of Texas at Arlington and a Ph.D in aerospace engineering from the University of Colorado Boulder. In 1994, Kalpana Chawla joined NASA's Johnson Space Center and became the first woman of Indian descent to fly in space. Her first space mission came in 1997 when she served as a mission specialist on the Space Shuttle Columbia during the STS-87 mission. In 2003, Kalpana Chawla was selected for the Space Shuttle Columbia mission STS-107. Tragically, the mission ended in disaster when the shuttle disintegrated upon re entry into Earth's atmosphere on February 1, 2003. Kalpana Chawla along with her six crewmates lost her life in the accident.

Kalpana Chawla's legacy however, extends far beyond the tragedy of her final mission. She is remembered as a pioneering astronaut who broke barriers and inspired millions around the world, especially in India. Her courage, determination and passion for exploration continue to serve as a beacon of hope for future generations of space explorers. In honor of her contributions to space exploration, Kalpana Chawla has been posthumously awarded numerous honors and accolades including the Congressional Space Medal of Honor, the NASA Space Flight Medal and the NASA Distinguished Service Medal.